A Local Table
The Choices Markets Cookbook

By Choices' own Desiree Nielsen RD & Antonio Cerullo

Celebrating a Local Table

Welcome to the first Choices Cookbook. The original idea for creating our own cookbook goes back many, many years. I believe we contemplated compiling recipes as early as 1990 (our first year of business). As often happens to great ideas, they hang around without definition until someone agrees to the hard work of seeing the project through from start to finish. In this case Desiree Nielsen, Choices' Registered Dietitian, stepped up and grabbed the project.

Desiree's concept for the cookbook was inspired by the abundance and year-round availability of local BC products—accordingly, she divided the book into four seasons. With that concept in mind she approached Choices' Executive Chef, Antonio Cerullo, to help her produce an original series of recipes. Antonio, ever inventive, created a set of superb and easy-to-follow recipes. During an early production meeting Desiree also floated the idea that nutritional information would help complete the book's content. We all agreed and hope you find her nutritional tips helpful and insightful.

The Cookbook's theme of using local ingredients year-round is an ideal way of underscoring our company's commitment to local farmers, growers and producers. We hope you are pleased to see photographs of a few of the local farmers we support. If you have any questions or comments about the book please email us at comments@choicesmarket.com.

Finally, I would like to thank the two main "movers and shakers" on this project. Desiree, we are deeply grateful for the energy and devotion you brought to this project. Antonio, without your culinary creativity and endless good cheer we never would have finished.

October 6, 2009

Mark Vickars
CEO, Choices Markets

Table of Contents

We wanted our cookbook to be no exception to our wellness philosophy;
we believe cooking should be a joy no matter what your dietary needs are! For your convenience,
each recipe is coded with coloured symbols to denote diet suitability:

Vegan   Vegetarian   Nut Free   Gluten Free   Detox Friendly

Sustainable Nutrition

Our health and the health of the planet are inextricably linked: it takes fresh water, clean and nutrient rich soil and favourable skies to grow nourishing food. Living in British Columbia, we are fortunate to have access to bountiful local harvests to lay on our dinner table. From local chevre and organic strawberries to wild sockeye salmon, healthful and flavourful foods are grown close to home. It is important to remember that these gifts are not self-sustaining - without responsible stewardship of our agricultural traditions, we risk this wealth.

Over the last two decades, concern for our food system has grown from simply ensuring global food supply to questioning the nutritional adequacy and ecological impact of the foods we eat.[3] Choosing high quality, whole foods and preparing them simply is a recipe for better health. Each time we lift our fork, we can make a conscious decision to eat sustainably.

A number of factors contribute to sustainable food systems: Where has the food been grown? What methods have been used? How much energy is needed to produce the food? What is the environmental impact of production and shipment? What is the impact of eating this food on our health?

This section contains tools to help support you on your journey toward a more sustainable table. Learn what is in season locally from our friends at Get Local BC; educate yourself about the benefits of eating local versus eating organic; discover how to reduce the carbon footprint of your meals and connect with Farm Folk/City Folk, a BC organization devoted to bringing eaters and producers together.

Get Local Vancouver Calendar

This guide is general information, availability can change due to weather.

 = **Greenhouse**

● = **Stored/Dried/Frozen**

VEGETABLES	J	F	M	A	M	J	J	A	S	O	N	D
Artichokes								■	■	■		
Asparagus					■	■						
Beans (Fresh)							■	■	■			
Beans (Dried)	■	■	■	■	■	■	■	■	■	■	■	■
Beets	●	●	●	●	●		■	■	■	■	■	
Broccoli							■	■	■	■	■	
Brussel Sprouts									■	■	■	■
Cabbage-Green & Red	●	●	●	●			■	■	■	■	■	●
Cabbage-Savoy & Red	■	■		●					■	■	■	■
Carrots	■	●	●	●	●		■	■	■	■	■	■
Cauliflower							■	■	■	■	■	
Celery							■	■	■	■		
Chard-Swiss						■	■	■	■	■		
Corn								■	■			
Cucumbers		▲	▲	▲	▲	▲	■	■	▲		▲	
Fennel (Bulb)							■	■	■	■		
Garlic (Fresh)							■	■				
Garlic (Dried)	■	■	■	■	■	■	■	■	■	■	■	■
Kale	■	■	■	■	■				■	■	■	■
Leeks	■	■	■	■					■	■	■	■
Lettuce					■	■	■	■	■	■		
Mustard Greens						■	■	■	■	■	■	
Onions-Green					■	■	■	■	■	■		
Onions-Red/Yellow	■	■	■	■	●	●	●	●	■	■	■	■
Parsnips			●	●	●				■	■	■	■
Peas						■	■					
Peppers			▲	▲	▲	▲	■	▲	▲	▲		
Potatoes - New						■	■	■				
Potatoes - Red, Russet, Yellow	●	●	●	●	●			■	■	■	■	■
Potatoes - White								■	■	■	■	■
Pumpkin									■	■	■	
Radishes				■	■	■	■	■	■	■		
Rhubarb-Field				■	■	■	■	■				
Rutabagas	●	●	●	●				■	■	■	■	■
Salad Greens					■	■	■	■	■	■		
Shallots	●	●	●	●	●	●	●	●		●	●	●
Spinach				■	■	■	■	■	■	■		
Squash-Summer							■	■	■			
Squash-Winter	●								■	■	■	■
Tomatoes			▲	▲	▲	▲	■	■	■	■	▲	
Turnips-White	●	●	●			■	■	■	■	■	■	■
Zucchini							■	■	■	■		

SEAFOOD

SEAFOOD	J	F	M	A	M	J	J	A	S	O	N	D
Clams	■	■	■	■	■	■	■	■	■	■	■	■
Cod: Pacific	■	■	■	■	■	■	■	■	■	■	■	■
Crab	■	■	■	■	■	■	■	■	■	■	■	■
Crab: Dungeness	■	■	■	■	■	■	■	■	■	■	■	■
Flounder/Sole: Pacific	■	■	■	■	■	■	■	■	■	■	■	■
Halibut: Pacific		■	■	■	■	■	■	■	■	■		
Herring			■									
Lingcod					■	■	■	■	■	■	■	
Mussels	■	■	■	■	■	■	■	■	■	■	■	■
Oysters: Pacific	■	■	■	■	■	■	■	■	■	■	■	■
Prawns: Jumbo	■	■	■	■	■	■	■	■	■	■	■	
Prawns: Spot	■	■			■	■						
Sablefish (Black Cod)	■	■	■	■	■	■				■	■	■
Salmon: Chinook/King/Spring						■	■	■	■			
Salmon: Chum								■	■	■		
Salmon: Coho (Northern)								■	■	■		
Salmon: Pink						■	■	■	■			
Salmon: Sockeye						■	■	■				
Sardines: Pacific									■	■		
Scallops	■	■	■	■	■	■				■	■	■
Shrimp: Side Stripe	■	■	■	■	■	■	■	■	■	■	■	■
Shrimp: West Coast	■	■	■	■	■	■	■	■	■	■	■	■
Spring Dogfish					■	■	■	■				
Tuna: Albacore							■	■	■	■		

Note: Frozen seafood is available year round.

FRUIT

FRUIT	J	F	M	A	M	J	J	A	S	O	N	D
Apples	■	■	■				■	■	■			■
Apricots							■	■				
Blackberries								■	■			
Blueberries							■	■	■			
Cherries (pie)							■	■				
Crab Apples								■	■	■		
Cranberries									■	■		
Currants							■	■				
Gooseberries						■	■					
Grapes									■			
Kiwi	■	■								■	■	■
Melons								■	■			
Nectarines							■	■				
Peaches								■	■			
Pears								■	■	■	■	■
Plums								■	■			
Prunes									■			
Quince										■	■	
Raspberries							■	■				
Rhubarb - Field				■	■	■	■					
Saskatoon Berries							■	■				
Strawberries						■	■	■				

SEAFOOD	J	F	M	A	M	J	J	A	S	O	N	D
Clams	●	●	●	●	●	●	●	●	●	●	●	●
Cod: Pacific	●	●	●	●	●	●	●	●	●	●	●	●
Crab	●	●	●	●	●	●	●	●	●	●	●	●
Crab: Dungeness	●	●	●	●	●	●	●	●	●	●	●	●
Flounder/Sole: Pacific	●	●	●	●	●	●	●	●	●	●	●	●
Halibut: Pacific			●	●	●	●	●	●	●	●	●	
Herring			●			●	●	●	●	●		
Lingcod					●	●	●	●	●	●	●	
Mussels	●	●	●	●	●	●	●	●	●	●	●	●
Oysters: Pacific	●	●	●	●	●	●	●	●	●	●	●	●
Prawns: Jumbo	●	●	●	●	●	●						
Prawns: Spot	●	●	●	●	●							
Sablefish (Black Cod)	●	●	●					●	●	●	●	●
Salmon: Chinook/King/Spring							●	●	●	●	●	●
Salmon: Chum								●	●	●		
Salmon: Coho (Northern)							●	●	●	●	●	
Salmon: Pink							●	●	●			
Salmon: Sockeye						●	●	●				
Sardines: Pacific									●	●	●	●
Scallops	●	●	●	●	●	●	●	●	●	●	●	●
Shrimp: Side Stripe	●	●	●	●	●	●	●	●	●	●	●	●
Shrimp: West Coast	●	●	●	●	●	●	●	●	●	●	●	●
Spring Dogfish	●	●	●	●			●	●	●	●	●	
Tuna: Albacore							●	●	●	●	●	●

Note: Frozen seafood is available year round.

FRUIT	J	F	M	A	M	J	J	A	S	O	N	D
Apples				●					●	●		
Apricots							●	●				
Blackberries							●	●				
Blueberries							●					
Cherries (pie)						●	●	●				
Crab Apples								●	●	●		
Cranberries									●	●		
Currants							●					
Gooseberries						●	●					
Grapes									●	●		
Kiwi		●									●	●
Melons									●	●		
Nectarines							●	●				
Peaches							●	●				
Pears									●	●	●	●
Plums								●	●			
Prunes								●	●	●		
Quince						●						
Raspberries						●	●					
Rhubarb - Field						●						
Saskatoon Berries						●	●					
Strawberries						●						

Get Local Okanagan Calendar

This guide is general information, availability can change due to weather.

 = **Greenhouse**

● = **Stored/Dried/Frozen**

Legend: ▲ = Greenhouse ● = Stored/Dried/Frozen ▓ = Available (green)

VEGETABLES	J	F	M	A	M	J	J	A	S	O	N	D
Artichokes								▓	▓	▓		
Asparagus				▓	▓							
Beans (Fresh)							▓	▓	▓			
Beans (Dried)	▓	▓	▓	▓	▓	▓	▓	▓	▓	▓	▓	▓
Beets	●	●	●	●	●	▓	▓	▓	▓	▓	▓	▓
Broccoli							▓	▓	▓	▓	▓	
Brussel Sprouts									▓	▓	▓	▓
Cabbage-Green & Red	●	●	●	●			▓	▓	▓	▓	▓	●
Cabbage-Savoy & Red	▓	▓	▓	●					▓	▓	▓	▓
Carrots	▓	●	●	●	●		▓	▓	▓	▓	▓	▓
Cauliflower							▓	▓	▓	▓	▓	
Celery							▓	▓	▓	▓		
Chard-Swiss				▓	▓	▓	▓	▓	▓	▓		
Corn								▓	▓			
Cucumbers				▲	▲	▓	▓	▓	▓			
Fennel (Bulb)								▓	▓	▓		
Garlic (Fresh)							▓	▓				
Garlic (Dried)	▓	▓	▓	▓	▓	▓	▓	▓	▓	▓	▓	▓
Kale			▓	▓	▓	▓	▓	▓	▓	▓	▓	
Leeks	▓	▓	▓						▓	▓	▓	▓
Lettuce				▲	▲	▓	▓	▓	▓	▓		
Mustard Greens						▓	▓	▓	▓	▓	▓	
Onions-Green						▓	▓	▓	▓	▓		
Onions-Red/Yellow				●	●	●		▓	▓	▓	▓	▓
Parsnips	▓	▓	●	●	●	▓						
Peas						▓	▓					
Peppers								▓	▓	▓		
Potatoes - New						▓	▓	▓				
Potatoes - Red, Russet, Yellow	●	●	●	●	●			▓	▓	▓	▓	▓
Potatoes - White								▓	▓	▓	▓	▓
Pumpkin									▓	▓	▓	
Radishes					▓	▓	▓	▓				
Rhubarb-Field						▓	▓					
Rutabagas	●	●	●	●			▓	▓	▓	▓	▓	▓
Salad Greens				▓	▓	▓	▓	▓	▓	▓	▓	
Shallots	●	●	●	●	●	●	●		●	●	●	●
Spinach				▓	▓	▓	▓	▓	▓	▓		
Squash-Summer							▓	▓	▓	▓		
Squash-Winter	●								▓	▓	▓	▓
Tomatoes				▲	▲	▓	▓	▓	▓	▓		
Turnips-White	●	●	●				▓	▓	▓	▓	▓	▓
Zucchini							▓	▓	▓	▓		

MEAT & DAIRY

MEAT & DAIRY	J	F	M	A	M	J	J	A	S	O	N	D
Dairy Products	■	■	■	■	■	■	■	■	■	■	■	■
Eggs	■	■	■	■	■	■	■	■	■	■	■	■
Beef	■	■	■	■	■	■	■	■	■	■	■	■
Buffalo	■	■	■	■	■	■	■	■	■	■	■	■
Chicken	■	■	■	■	■	■	■	■	■	■	■	■
Duck	■	■	■	■	■	■	■	■	■	■	■	■
Goat	■	■	■	■	■	■	■	■	■	■	■	■
Lamb	■	■	■	■	■	■	■	■	■	■	■	■
Ostrich	■	■	■	■						■	■	■
Pheasant	■		■	■	■	■	■	■	■		■	■
Pork	■	■	■	■	■	■	■	■	■	■	■	■
Rabbit	■	■	■	■	■	■	■	■	■	■	■	■
Turkey	■	■	■	■	■	■	■	■	■	■	■	■

Note: Frozen meat products are available year round.

HERBS

HERBS	J	F	M	A	M	J	J	A	S	O	N	D
Bay Leaves	■	■	■	■	■	■	■	■	■	■	■	■
Basils			■	■	■	■	■	■				
Chives				■	■				■	■		
Chives-garlic			■	■	■					■		
Chervil	■	■				■	■	■		■	■	■
Cilantro	■	■	■	■		■	■	■	■		■	■
Dill -leaf					■	■	■	■	■			
Dill-seed							■	■	■			
Epazote					■	■	■	■	■	■		
Fennel-leaf			■	■	■	■	■	■	■			
Fennel -Seed							■	■	■	■		
Lavender						■	■	■				
Lemon Grass					■	■	■	■	■			
Lemon verbena					■	■	■	■	■	■		
Marjoram- sweet						■	■	■	■			
Mints				■	■	■	■	■	■	■		
Oreganoes			■	■	■	■	■	■	■	■		
Parsleys			■	■	■	■	■	■	■	■	■	
Rosemarys	■	■	■	■	■	■	■	■	■	■	■	■
Sages	■	■	■	■	■	■	■	■	■	■	■	
Savory-summer					■	■	■	■				
Savory-winter	■	■	■	■					■	■	■	■
Shiso						■	■	■				
Sorrel			■	■	■					■	■	
Tarragon-french	■	■	■	■	■	■	■	■	■	■	■	
Thymes	■	■	■	■	■	■	■	■	■	■	■	■

ETC.

ETC.	J	F	M	A	M	J	J	A	S	O	N	D
Grains								■	■	■		
Honey	●	●	●	●	●	■	■	■	■	●	●	●
Mushrooms	■	■	■	■	■	■	■	■	■	■	■	■
Nuts	●	●	●	●	●	●	●	●	■	■	●	●

MEAT & DAIRY

MEAT & DAIRY	J	F	M	A	M	J	J	A	S	O	N	D
Dairy Products	■	■	■	■	■	■	■	■	■	■	■	■
Eggs	■	■	■	■	■	■	■	■	■	■	■	■
Beef	■	■	■	■	■	■	■	■	■	■	■	■
Buffalo	■	■	■	■	■	■	■	■	■	■	■	■
Chicken	■	■	■	■	■	■	■	■	■	■	■	■
Duck	■	■	■	■	■	■	■	■	■	■	■	■
Goat	■	■	■	■	■	■	■	■	■	■	■	■
Lamb	■	■	■	■	■	■	■	■	■	■	■	■
Ostrich					■	■	■	■	■		■	■
Pheasant	■									■	■	■
Pork	■		■	■	■	■	■	■	■	■	■	■
Rabbit	■	■	■	■	■	■	■	■	■	■	■	■
Turkey	■	■	■	■	■	■	■	■	■	■	■	■

Note: Frozen meat products are available year round.

HERBS

HERBS	J	F	M	A	M	J	J	A	S	O	N	D
Bay Leaves				■	■	■	■	■	■			
Basils					■	■	■	■	■	■		
Chives				■	■	■	■	■	■	■		
Chives-garlic				■	■	■	■	■	■	■		
Chervil				■	■	■			■	■		
Cilantro				■	■	■	■	■	■			
Dill -leaf				■	■	■	■	■	■			
Dill-seed						■	■	■	■			
Epazote					■	■	■	■	■			
Fennel-leaf				■	■	■	■					
Fennel -Seed							■	■	■	■		
Lavender						■	■	■				
Lemon Grass						■	■	■	■			
Lemon verbena						■	■	■	■	■		
Marjoram- sweet					■	■	■	■	■	■		
Mints				■	■	■	■	■	■	■		
Oreganoes				■	■	■	■	■	■	■		
Parsleys				■	■	■	■	■	■	■		
Rosemarys				■	■	■	■	■	■	■		
Sages				■	■	■	■	■	■	■		
Savory-summer					■	■	■	■	■	■		
Savory-winter				■	■	■	■	■	■	■		
Shiso					■	■	■	■				
Sorrel				■	■	■			■	■		
Tarragon-french				■	■	■	■	■	■	■		
Thymes				■	■	■	■	■	■	■		

MISC.

MISC.	J	F	M	A	M	J	J	A	S	O	N	D
Grains								■	■	■		
Honey	●	●	●	●	●	■	■	■	■	●	●	●
Mushrooms	■	■	■	■	■	■	■	■	■	■	■	
Nuts	●	●	●	●	●	●	●	●	■	■	●	●

Go Local or Go Organic?

Buying local and organic foods is a powerful tool in supporting a sustainable food supply.
As awareness of the benefits of locally produced food grows, so does the debate over which is most important: to be local or organic? While a definitive answer may not exist, what follows is a discussion to help you make an informed decision for you and your family.

In British Columbia, our most valuable agricultural land lies within urban environments.
Local food production must be preserved to secure a livelihood for a new generation of farmers. If a new generation abandons existing farmland, we risk losing it to urban development. Buying local food helps preserve local farmland and supports local jobs.

Buying local also reduces the carbon footprint of our meals and improves the nutrient density of our food. Food travelling long distances must be picked before it is ripe – before full development of nutrients can occur. Long travel times further degrade nutrient levels[6,7] and the addition of mould and fungus inhibitors are required to survive long journeys.

Most of the world's water is used for agriculture[2] and food is second only to transportation in producing carbon emissions.[4] Air pollution destroys crops and impacts human lives – yet flying produce across the globe puts tonnes of carbon emissions into the air. A 2003 Ontario survey of a representative food basket purchased at a local supermarket revealed that foods travelled an average of 5364 kilometres from field to store.[1] Local foods go a long way towards a smaller carbon footprint for our families.

In a perfect world, an abundance of affordable, local and organic food would be available year round. Unfortunately, seasonality and growing conditions will not allow us to produce 100% of our food needs[5]. Greenhouse technology allows us to enjoy a longer growing season but it may not be energy efficient. In addition, many foods near and dear to our heart are not grown locally, including chocolate, spices and coffee.

The benefits of organics are well documented: intensive agriculture strips nutrients from the soil and relies on chemical fertilizers to feed growing plants and pesticides to protect the delicate crops. Organic foods are better for the air, the water and for those who harvest them. Organic farming methods also nourish the soil so that the foods grown within them nourish us in kind. In addition, organic standards prohibit the use of GMO seeds to preserve genetic integrity of our food[2]. Encouraging organic production methods abroad and here at home will ensure a cleaner, healthier environment for future generations.

Sustainable Nutrition:
10 Steps Towards a
Smaller Carbon Footprint

1. Grow your own! It doesn't get more local or natural than your own backyard or patio. Dig in, get dirty and enjoy the freshest produce possible.

2. Ban the bottle. Water is one of our greatest natural resources and clean drinking water should be available to all. When we buy bottled water, we are not only paying for something that is provided for free but also wasting valuable energy on packaging and shipping the product across the globe. Purchase a filter jug and reusable metal water bottle instead.

3. Avoid buying individually packed items. Single serve packages are more expensive and create excess waste. Buy family-sized containers and portion your food into reusable containers for packed lunches and snacks – it only takes a minute to do!

4. Eat local. Picked at the peak of freshness, local foods support the local economy and have a smaller carbon footprint than imports.

5. Eat organic. Organic foods preserve the health of our soils, air and ground water while preserving the genetic integrity of our food. Eating organic foods also reduces your family's exposure to artificial preservatives, colours and flavouring agents.

6. Choose sustainable seafood. With the environment and fisheries at risk, choose only seafood that is certified sustainable by a respected third party such as OceanWise.

7. Compost your food scraps. Composting not only helps reduce food waste but it provides gorgeously rich fertilizer for your backyard garden. Even condo dwellers can compost thanks to the new "counter top" bins.

8. Go meatless more often. Livestock production accounts for the vast majority of water and land required to feed North Americans[2]. Eating meatless meals a few times a week is lean, green and good for you!

9. Play fair. Many of our most treasured foods – sugar, cocoa, tea and coffee – are produced by vulnerable populations in the developing world. Look for Fair Trade products to ensure a safe and sustainable livelihood for those who provide us with these delights.

10. Eat healthy meat from happy animals. Organically raised free range meats ensure the highest standards of animal husbandry and the least environmental impact possible[8].

1. Lang, T. and Heasman, M.. Food Wars: the global battle for mouths, minds and markets. Earthscan London: 2004

2. Food Secure Vancouver Baseline Report. Vancouver Food Policy Council: March 2009. Accessed on July 6, 2009 at http://www.vancouverfoodpolicycouncil.ca/sites/default/files/FoodSecureVancouverBaselineStudy.pdf

3. The Benefits of Eating Locally. Get Local BC. Accessed on July 3, 2009 at http://www.getlocalbc.org/en/

4. Eat Well and Save the Planet! A guide for consumers on how to eat greener, healthier and more ethical food. Sustain: December 2007. Accessed on July 6, 2009 at http://www.sustainweb.org/pdf/SFG_Consumers_1pp.pdf

5. Pazderka, C., Rowan, A. and Enno Tamm, E.. The Green Guide to David Suzuki's Nature Challenge. David Suzuki Foundation: Accessed on June 26, 2009 at http://www.davidsuzuki.org/files/WOL/GreenGuide.pdf

6. Brower, M. and Leon, W. The Consumers Guide to Effective Environmental Choices: practical advice from the union of concerned scientists. Three Rivers Press New York: 1999

7. Bentley, S and Barker R. Fighting Global Warming at the Farmer's Market: the role of local food systems in reducing greenhouse gas emissions. Foodshare Toronto: April 2005. Accessed on June 26, 2009 at http://www.foodshare.net/resource/files/ACF230.pdf

8. Certified Organic Associations of BC. Accessed on July 9, 2009 at http://www.certifiedorganic.bc.ca/

Spring

Ah, spring! Filled with the promise of longer days, green starts to emerge from the grey and early flowers bloom with a riot of colour against the gloomy landscape. Springtime eating bridges the seasons; local winter produce that lent itself to rich meals to battle the still cool days is replaced with all things green and fresh to awaken our imaginations. Spring poses the greatest challenge to a locavore as the root cellar is wearing thin after a long winter and we crave the freshness of summer's bounty. While most of Canada is still under snow, a few hardy species peek their heads out of the earth here in BC and signal a return to all that is good and local: fiddleheads and asparagus are among the pioneers that will sustain us now. We will wait until the later days of spring before we see celery, spinach, new potatoes, radishes, strawberries and rhubarb.

Creamy Maple Rice Pudding

Ingredients

1/2 cup	Kakuho rice or short grain rice
3 1/2 cups	Natura unsweetened soy milk
1 piece	organic lemon rind
4 tbsp	Luc Bergeron Organic maple syrup
1	vanilla pod or 1 tsp vanilla extract

Serves 6

Nutrition Facts per Serving:
Calories 140, Carbohydrate 24g, Protein 5g, Fat 2g, Fibre 2g, Sodium 30mg

Method

1. In a very heavy saucepan, bring all ingredients to a boil then reduce to simmer, while stirring constantly on medium heat for approximately 35 minutes.

2. Chill and serve.

Delicious served with seasonal fruit salads or berry compote.

Italian Brown Rice with Arugula Pesto

Ingredients

1	yellow pepper
1	bunch fresh arugula
1 cup	freshly grated Pecorino Romano cheese
1/4 cup	Omega Nutrition extra virgin olive oil
2	cloves garlic
1 tsp	black pepper
1/4 cup	walnuts (optional)
1 cup	short grain brown rice
1 tsp	sea salt
4	Roma tomatoes

Serves 6

Nutrition Facts per Serving:
Calories 410, Carbohydrates 35g, Protein 17g, Fat 24g, Fibre 3g, Sodium 1190mg

Method

1. Roast pepper on open flame BBQ or in 450° F oven until all skin has completely browned. While still hot, put aside in a bowl covered with a plate and let it sit for 15 minutes before peeling and removing seeds.

2. Once pepper has completely cooled, blend in a food processor with garlic, arugula, olive oil, pepper and add the cheese last. If using walnuts, add before the cheese.

3. Cook brown rice according to instructions on package. Mix hot rice with pesto and diced tomatoes. For a cold rice dish, allow rice to cool before mixing with pesto.

The pesto is also delicious with pasta, on canapés, or blended with mayo

Baked Brie and Sun Dried Figs

Ingredients

1/3 cup	Omega Nutrition Balsamic Vinegar
1/4 cup	Luc Bergeron Organic Maple Syrup
7	dried figs, finely diced
250 g	brie (2 small or 1 medium)

Serves 4

Nutrition Facts per Serving:
Calories 300, Carbohydrate 23g Protein 13g, Fat 17g, Fibre1g, Sodium 400mg

Method

1. Preheat oven to 400° F.

2. In a small saucepan, bring balsamic vinegar and maple syrup to a boil. Lower to simmer and add finely diced figs.

3. After 5 minutes, consistency of sauce should be similar to honey. Remove from heat.

4. Divide brie in half horizontally to produce two wheels.

5. Place brie wheels on nonstick baking sheet, rind down. Divide fig compote evenly on tops and bake for approximately 6 minutes or until brie starts melting.

6. Serve hot with crusty baguette or your favourite bread.

Mediterranean Halibut Bites with Pesto Dressing

Halibut Ingredients

450 g	halibut fillets, from Classic Smokehouse
3 tbsp	capers
1 tsp	black pepper
1/2 tsp	salt
4	cloves garlic
2 tsp	oregano
2 tsp	fennel seeds
3 tbsp	Omega Nutrition extra virgin olive oil

Pesto Dressing Ingredients

4 tbsp	mayonnaise
2 tbsp	pesto
1 tbsp	red wine vinegar
2 tbsp	Omega Nutrition Extra virgin olive oil

Serves 6 (3 bites per person)

Nutrition Facts per Serving:
Calories 220, Carbohydrates 3g, Protein 17g, Fat 15g, Fibre 1g, Sodium 410mg

Method

1. Prepare the dressing: combine all dressing ingredients and set aside.

2. For the halibut bites, chop halibut into small pieces.

3. Combine halibut and all remaining ingredients, except olive oil, in food processor. Process until ingredients form an even mixture.

4. Form into 18 balls, approximately the size of a quarter.

5. In a non-stick pan, heat oil on medium heat and cook fish until golden brown.

Can be served hot or cold with mixed greens and the pesto dressing.

Focus on Nutrition: Capers are not seeds or fruits but are actually the immature bud of the caper flower. Caper berries, on the other hand, are the fruit of the caper bush.

Citrus and Wild Mushroom Fettuccine

Ingredients

450 g	Prairie Harvest Organic Fettuccine or San Zenone Brown Rice Fettuccine
400 g	fresh oyster mushrooms, sliced lengthwise
2	cloves garlic, sliced
1/2 cup	fresh lemon juice (approx 2 large juicy lemons)
1/2 cup	dry white wine or water
2 tbsp	fresh sage, chopped
1/4 cup + 3 tbsp	Omega Nutrition extra virgin olive oil
1/4 tbsp	black pepper
1 tsp	sea salt
1 cup	freshly grated Parmigiano Reggiano cheese, omit for vegan recipe

Serves 6 hungry people – 12 as a light first course

Nutrition Facts per Serving:
Calories 620, Carbohydrate 64g, Protein 25g, Fat 29g, Fibre 5g, Sodium 310mg

Method

1. In a heavy saucepan, bring lemon juice, white wine, garlic, olive oil, sage, black pepper and salt to a boil.

2. When boiling, add mushrooms and lower heat to simmer, simmering until reduced by half.

3. In a large pot of boiling salted water, cook fettuccine to al dente (as per package instructions) and strain.

4. Toss pasta with mushroom sauce and parmesan cheese.

Focus on Nutrition:
Parmesan cheese is a bone booster:
just one tablespoon has
60 mg of calcium.

Turkey Breast
with Grapefruit and Mint

Ingredients

2 tbsp	Omega Nutrition extra virgin olive oil
700 g	JD Farms Specialty turkey breast, boneless and skinless, diced
100 g	dried cranberries
1	clove garlic, chopped
1/2	lemon, juiced
1	large grapefruit, cubed
3 tbsp	fresh mint, chopped
1 tsp	salt (optional)

Serves 4

Nutrition Facts per Serving:
Calories 370, Carbohydrate 28g, Protein 42g, Fat 10g, Fibre 3g, Sodium 700mg

---

Method

1. In a large frying pan, heat oil and sauté turkey cubes.

2. When brown but not fully cooked (3 – 4 minutes), add dried cranberries and cook for 2 – 3 more minutes.

3. Add chopped garlic, lemon juice and sauté for another minute.

4. Add cubed grapefruit and continue sautéing until juices start reducing.

5. Add salt (optional) and fresh chopped mint.

Focus on Nutrition:
The scent of limonene, a primary
component of grapefruit oil,
may help to control appetite.

Mushroom and Mustard Seed Salad

Ingredients

3/4 lb	fresh organic brown mushrooms, thinly sliced
1	stalk celery, finely sliced
1 tsp	fresh rosemary, chopped
2 tsp	yellow mustard seeds
2 tsp	black mustard seeds
3 tbsp	Omega Nutrition apple cider vinegar
1/2 tsp	sea salt
1	clove garlic, chopped
3 tbsp	Omega Nutrition High O Sunflower Oil

Serves 6 as a side dish

Nutrition Facts per Serving:
Calories 90, Carbohydrate 3g, Protein 2g, Fat 8g, Fibre 1g, Sodium 170mg

Method

1. Soak mustard seeds in vinegar, overnight if possible.

2. Temper salt into vinegar and mustard seeds. Add oil.

3. Combine all ingredients, including mustard mixture, in bowl and mix.

This salad can be consumed immediately or refrigerated for up to 24 hours. The raw mushrooms' consistency will change when dressed and refrigerated.

Focus on Nutrition: Mushrooms contain a vitamin D precursor, which may help strengthen your bones

Stinking Rows Garlic Farm
Salmon Arm BC

The Harper family has been involved with agriculture for over 100 years. For the last 11 years, Brian and Alana Harper, together with their adult children, have specialized in growing premium garlic on their small farm nestled in picturesque Salmon Arm, 5 hours northeast of Vancouver.

All of the garlic produced by the Harpers is grown without the use of pesticides. The family takes pride in using environmentally sustainable and responsible farming methods. Weeds are controlled using old-fashioned traditional methods and are either pulled by hand, removed with gardening tools or tilled with a machine.

The Harpers motto, "Grown with pride from our family to yours," aligns closely with Choices Markets, philosophy. As it is our goal to support BC growers everywhere, Choices Markets is proud to be a partner with Stinking Rows Garlic Farm, bringing our customers the Harpers' finest garlic every fall.

Portobello Melt

Ingredients

2	large Portobello mushrooms
1	small wheel of "blue" brie (or substitute regular brie)
2 tbsp	Omega Nutrition extra virgin olive oil
3	garlic cloves
3 tbsp	fresh rosemary, chopped
1	lemon rind, grated
dash	salt

Serves 2 as an entree

Nutrition Facts per Serving:
Calories 370, Carbohydrates 7g, Protein 16g, Fat 32g, Fibre 2g, Sodium 65mg

Method

1. Preheat oven to 375° F.

2. In a metal skillet or cast iron pan, heat olive oil on medium-high heat.

3. Remove stems from mushrooms and set aside; place mushroom caps in pan smooth side up and cook for 5 – 8 minutes.

4. Flip and cook for 2 – 3 more minutes then remove and place in baking dish, smooth side down.

5. Chop stems and garlic and place in hot skillet, adding small amounts of water (2 – 3 tbsp at a time). Cook for approximately 5 minutes.

6. Add rosemary, lemon rind and salt; cook until mixture starts browning and drying.

7. Top mushroom caps with mixture and bake for 8 – 10 minutes.

8. Remove caps from oven. Cut brie lengthwise forming two round wheels of cheese and place half a wheel on top of each cap, rind side down.

9. Return to oven for 3 – 5 minutes, just enough to melt the cheese. Serve hot.

Works well as vegetarian main or as a sandwich filling.

To serve 4 as an appetizer, cut Portobello melts in half and serve on baby greens.

Pumpkin Seed Hummus

Ingredients

2	small bulbs of garlic (or 1 large bulb), roasted
2	cans organic chick peas (540 ml), rinsed and drained
3 tbsp	Omega Nutrition pumpkin seed butter
100 ml	lemon juice
100 ml	Omega Nutrition extra virgin olive oil
1 tsp	sea salt
1/4 tsp	ground cumin
1/4 tsp	ground coriander
1/4 tsp	ground black pepper, optional

Serves 20 as a snack or spread

Nutrition Facts per Serving:
Calories 125, Carbohydrate 14g, Protein 3.5g, Fat 6.5g, Fibre 3g, Sodium 250mg

Method

1. To roast garlic, preheat oven to 375° F and wrap garlic in tin foil. Place garlic in oven for 40 minutes until garlic bulbs are soft and caramelized.

2. In food processor, blend garlic, pumpkin seed butter, spices, salt and lemon juice.

3. When this mixture is pureed, add chick peas. Using medium/fast speed, process while drizzling in oil slowly, until mixture is smooth.

Serve with favorite raw veggies or as a spread on sandwiches. Hummus will keep in the fridge for 4 days.

 *Focus on Nutrition: Pumpkin seeds are rich in omega 3 fatty acids, which help to calm inflammation in the body.*

Spinach and Feta Frittata

Ingredients

3 tbsp	Omega Nutrition extra virgin olive oil
1 small	onion, chopped
1 clove	garlic, chopped
145 g	package of fresh spinach (5oz)
113 g	Happy Days goat feta, crumbled
6	eggs
pinch	salt

Serves 4

Nutrition Facts per Serving:
Calories 280, Carbohydrate 8g, Protein 12g, Fat 23g, Fibre 3g, Sodium 410mg

Method

1. Preheat broiler.

2. Heat oil in frying pan; add onions and garlic. As onions start to brown, add spinach and cover temporarily to allow spinach to wilt faster, about 1 – 2 minutes.

3. Remove lid and sauté spinach for 3 – 4 minutes until fully cooked.

4. In a medium bowl, beat eggs lightly with a fork until mixed. Add feta and mix.

5. Add cooked spinach mixture to egg mixture in the bowl and return to hot frying pan.

6. Cook for 4 – 6 minutes at medium heat then cover, cooking for two more minutes.

7. To finish, place under pre-heated broiler element for 4 – 5 minutes making sure that top part of frittata cooks. Serve hot or eat leftovers cold next day with a side salad.

 *Focus on Nutrition: Extra Virgin Olive Oil comes from the first cold pressing of the olives and contains more antioxidants than later pressings.*

Swiss Chard Wraps with Yogurt Pesto

Ingredients

1	bunch Swiss chard, leaves and stalks
1	small carrot
2	Portobello mushrooms
1	stalk celery
1	small leek
2 tbsp	fresh parsley, chopped
1 tsp	chili powder
1/4 tsp	black pepper
2 tsp +1/4 tsp	salt
2 tbsp	Omega Nutrition extra virgin olive oil
1/2 cup	plain Olympic Organic 2% yogurt
2 tbsp	pesto
1/2 cup	white wine

Serves 6

Nutrition Facts per Serving:
Calories 100, Carbohydrates 6g, Protein 1g, Fat 7g, Fibre 2g, Sodium 420mg

Method

1. Preheat oven to 400° F.

2. Cut chard stalks, carrots, celery and leeks in julienne style (long, matchstick width).

3. Quickly blanch (30 seconds) chard leaves in 4 litres of boiling water with 2 tsp salt.

4. In a heavy frying pan, brown leeks and chard stalks. Add chopped mushrooms, 1/4 tsp salt and pepper and stir fry for 5 minutes. Next, add celery and carrots, stir frying on medium high for 10 more minutes.

5. Add white wine and chili powder and cook until all liquid has evaporated.

6. To assemble, place a couple of teaspoons of cooked vegetable mixture on stem end of a chard leaf, folding outside edges in, and then roll. Place in a pyrex dish and bake for 15 minutes.

7. Mix yogurt with a pinch of salt and pesto for dipping. Serve hot or cold.

Focus on Nutrition: Greens like Swiss chard are packed with antioxidants, fibre and vitamin K, a bone building nutrient.

Tofu and Shiitake Stir Fry

Ingredients

350 g	Soyganic firm organic tofu, diced
400 g	fresh shiitake mushrooms, stem removed and thinly sliced
27 g	dried shiitake or mixed mushrooms (2 packets)
100 ml	sherry
2 tbsp	corn starch
2	limes, juiced
2 tbsp	Luc Bergeron Organic maple syrup
6 tbsp	toasted sesame oil
1 tbsp	fresh ginger, grated
5	garlic cloves, sliced
1 lb	frozen edamame beans
4 tbsp	tamari (gluten free or regular)
4 tbsp	parsley, chopped
2 cups	water
pinch	salt

Serves 4

Nutrition Facts per Serving:
Calories 400, Carbohydrate 28g, Protein 15g, Fat 27g, Fibre 3g, Sodium 1000mg

Method

1. Soak dried mushrooms in 2 cups of boiled water for at least half an hour. Remove mushrooms from water and chop, reserving both water and mushrooms.

2. Marinate tofu with corn starch, 100 ml sherry, lime juice, maple syrup, ginger, and tamari for at least 30 minutes or overnight.

3. In a wok or large frying pan, heat 2 tbsp sesame oil on medium-high and sauté fresh shiitakes, stirring constantly for approximately 4 – 5 minutes.

4. Add garlic and continue cooking for 3 – 4 more minutes. Next, add 2 tbsp parsley and sauté for 2 more minutes. Add 100 ml of sherry; chopped dried mushrooms and pinch of salt. Sauté until all liquid has evaporated.

5. Remove mushroom mixture from wok and return wok to medium high heat with 2 tbsp sesame oil. Heat lightly and add frozen edamame beans, cooking for 8 – 10 minutes. Add half cup of reserved mushroom water and cook until water has almost evaporated.

6. Add mushroom mixture, stir for 1 minute and remove from wok.

7. Return wok again to medium-high heat, adding 2 tbsp sesame oil. With a slotted spoon, remove tofu from marinade and place in hot wok. Sauté for 5 – 7 minutes; add remaining marinade, mushroom water and parsley. Return edamame and mushroom mixture to wok and mix.

Focus on Nutrition:
Shiitakes have a unique compound
called lentinan which may help to
boost your immune system.

Carrot and Zucchini "Flowers" and Shitake Caps Stuffed with Goat Cheese

Ingredients

1	head Garlic
2 +1/2 +1/2	Omega Nutrition Extra virgin olive oil
2	Organic carrots, washed, unpeeled if possible
2	medium zucchini
6	medium sized shitake mushrooms
1 tbsp	fresh rosemary, chopped
1/2 tsp + a few pinches	sea salt
1 tsp	pepper, coarsely ground
1 tbsp	Omega Nutrition Pumpkin seed oil
3 tsp	Omega Nutrition Pumpkin seed oil
250g	Happy Days soft goat cheese
6	small handfuls mixed baby greens
1 tbsp	Omega Nutrition Balsamic vinegar

Serves 6

Nutrition Facts per Serving:
Calories 150, Carbohydrate 6g, Protein 5g, Fat 12g, Fibre 1g, Sodium 200mg

Method

1. Preheat oven to 375° F. Cut the top off of the head of garlic and lightly brush the garlic with 1/2 tbsp olive oil. Bake for 25 minutes. Once garlic is roasted, remove and increase oven temperature to 400° F.

2. Meanwhile, cut the tip off the bottom of the carrot to make the end flat. Starting about 1 inch from the bottom of the carrot, make a scallop shaped cut towards the centre of the carrot, at a 45 degree downward angle. Continue making scalloped shaped cuts around the perimeter of the carrot, making a small bowl shaped carrot "flower". Once the first flower is complete, cut the end off the bottom of the carrot to make it flat. Repeat this process to make the remainder of the carrot flowers. Use the same procedure for the zucchini. Reserve all carrot and zucchini trimmings for later use.

3. Blanch carrot "flowers" in salted water for 3 minutes and zucchini for 1.5 minutes. For a softer vegetable, cook longer. Remove carrot and zucchini pieces from the water and place them in an ice water bath. Strain and let dry. Remove the stems from the shitake mushrooms and quickly pan fry caps for 1 minute in 1/2 tbsp olive oil.

4. In a food processor, combine 2 cloves of roasted garlic, rosemary, 1/2 tsp salt, pepper, 1 tbsp pumpkin seed oil and the reserved carrot and zucchini trimmings from step 2. Process until well chopped. Add goat cheese and blend until uniform.

5. Place the mixture in a piping bag with a small tip. If you don't have a piping bag, fill the corner of a small zipper bag with about 2 tbsp cheese mixture. Cut a small hole the diameter of a ball point pen in the corner. Fill carrot & zucchini flowers and shitake mushroom caps with the cheese mixture.

6. Bake for 10 minutes

7. In a small bowl, combine Balsamic vinegar, 2 tbsp olive oil and a few pinches of sea salt. Use to dress the mixed greens.

Serve the stuffed vegetables on small plates with a handful of mixed greens. Drizzle each plate with approximately 1/2 tsp of pumpkin seed oil and small amounts of roasted garlic.

Pasta and Chopped Veggie Salad

Ingredients

16 oz	San Zenone rice fusilli pasta (1 pkg) (or any short variety of pasta)
1	clove garlic, chopped
1	can baby corn, cut in halves
1	small zucchini, cubed
1	small bell pepper, cubed
1	small bunch asparagus, cut into small rounds
1	green onion, chopped
3 tbsp	lemon juice
1 tbsp	lemon zest
2 tbsp	chives, chopped
2 tbsp	fresh basil, chopped
200 g	cheddar cheese, shredded (optional)
1	bottle gluten free oil based salad dressing (236 ml)

Serves 8

Nutrition Facts per Serving:
Calories 360, Carbohydrate 57g, Protein 14g, Fat 10g, Fibre 5g, Sodium 290mg.
Note: nutrition information will vary widely based on dressing used.

Method

1. Cook pasta in large pot of boiling water, uncovered, until just tender. Drain and rinse under cold water.

2. Boil or steam asparagus until just tender.

3. In a large bowl, combine all ingredients and mix. Cover and chill for 1 hour.

Beef Salmonato

Sirloin Ingredients

3 l	water
2	carrots, halved
1	celery stalk, halved
1	medium onion, quartered
1 tsp	fennel seeds
3 or 4	peppercorns
1	whole clove garlic
1.5 lbs	Diamond Willow Organic whole beef top sirloin, outside round or eye of round (700 g)

Salmonato Sauce Ingredients

2	egg yolks
1/2	lemon, juiced
2 tbsp	capers
1/2 cup	Omega Nutrition extra virgin olive oil
1/2	can Raincoast Trading pink salmon
2 tbsp	lox or smoked salmon trim from Classic Smokehouse
4 tbsp	reserved stock made with beef

Serves 4 - 6

Nutrition Facts per Serving:
Calories (1/4 of recipe) 680,
Carbohydrates 8g, Protein
45g, Fat 51g, Fibre 2g,
odium 590mg

Sirloin Method

1. In a 5 quart pot, bring first seven ingredients to a boil, wait to add beef.

2. When liquid has reached a boil, lower heat and simmer. Let simmer for 15 minutes, then add whole beef.

3. Continue to simmer for 45 minutes then remove from heat. Allow beef and stock to cool. Remove beef from stock and refrigerate until completely cold.

4. Remove beef from fridge and slice as thinly as possible. Lay slices on a large serving platter or arrange on individual plates and cover with salmon sauce.

Salmonato sauce Method

1. In a blender mix egg yolks, lemon juice and capers for about 2 minutes.

2. Very slowly add olive oil while continuing to blend.

3. Drain canned salmon and along with lox blend with mixture until smooth.

4. Slowly add cold stock, continuing to blend until ingredients are completely mixed.

Leftovers are excellent as a sandwich filling. Soup stock can be refrigerated or frozen for later use. Serves 4 as a main course or 6 as an appetizer

Turkey and Veggie Meatballs

Ingredients

1	bunch spinach
1 tbsp	Omega Nutrition extra virgin olive oil
1	small onion, finely chopped
1	medium zucchini, shredded
1lb	lean ground JD Farms specialty turkey (450 g)
1	loosely packed cup freshly grated Parmiggiano Reggiano
1/4 tsp	salt

Ingredients Sauce

1	large can diced tomatoes
1	clove garlic
2 tbsp	Omega Nutrition extra virgin olive oil

Serves 6

Nutrition Facts per Serving:
Calories (1/6 recipe, without pasta) 290, Carbohydrates 13g, Protein 22g, Fat 17g, Fibre 3g, Sodium 650mg

Method

1. Preheat oven to 350° F.

2. After washing the spinach, blanch in boiling water. Strain, cool and set aside.

3. In a small frying pan over medium heat, heat olive oil and brown onion.

4. Add zucchini, spinach and salt; continue to sauté for 15 minutes. Remove from heat and cool.

5. Purée zucchini and spinach mixture in food processor.

6. In a large bowl, combine purée with turkey and cheese, mixing well.

7. Form at least 16 – 18 meatballs, approximately 1.5 in/3cm in diameter. Place on non-stick or greased baking sheet and bake for 20 minutes.

8. In a large saucepan over medium heat, heat olive oil with garlic clove.

9. When the garlic is sizzling, carefully add the can of tomatoes and simmer for 15 minutes.

10. Add meatballs and continue simmering for another 15 minutes.

11. Serve with 500 g of your favorite pasta. The meat balls are also wonderful on their own for 4 adults.

Gluten Free Vegan Chocolate Fudge Cake

Ingredients

1/2 cup	Anita's Organic buckwheat flour
1/4 cup	Omega Nutrition virgin coconut oil
1/4 cup +2 tbsp	Mum's Original hemp seeds
1 cup	organic crispy rice cereal
1/4 cup	Camino Cuisine golden cane sugar
2	packs Camino Cuisine semi-sweet chocolate chips (227g)
210 ml	organic coconut milk (7 oz)

Serves 12

Nutrition Facts per Serving:
Calories 350, Carbohydrates 26g, Protein 3g, Fat 26g, Fibre 2g, Sodium 25mg

Method

1. Preheat oven to 350° F.

2. In food processor, combine buckwheat flour, coconut oil, 1/4 cup of hemp seeds, crispy rice and sugar. Blend until smooth.

3. Press mixture into bottom of 6 inch spring form pan, packing tightly. Bake for 18 minutes. Remove from oven and cool completely.

4. Place chocolate chips and coconut milk in a steel bowl. Place on top of a simmering pot of water and mix carefully as it melts over the heat—do not overheat.

5. When mixture is silky and smooth, transfer into spring form pan while still hot. Sprinkle remaining 2 tbsp of hemp seeds on top and refrigerate overnight.

6. Remove from spring pan, slice and garnish as desired.

Due to the richness of this great dessert, a very small slice goes a long way. What better way to celebrate Celiac Awareness Month!

 *This decadent recipe is a "better for you" alternative to cheesecakes or tortes made with whipping cream.*

Tuna and Brown Rice Wrap

Ingredients

1/2 cup	short grain brown rice, rinsed
1 cup	water
1	medium carrot, grated
1/2 cup	Olympic Organic plain 2% yogurt
1/2	lime, juiced
1/2 tsp	salt
3 tbsp	Omega Nutrition extra virgin olive oil
1/2 tsp	curry powder
1	can Raincoast Trading Albacore tuna, drained (170 g)
1	ripe tomato, diced small
1	pack onion sprouts
	pepper if desired
6	wraps of your choice

Serves 6

Nutrition Facts per Serving:
Calories (without wrap) 160,
Carbohydrates 14g, Protein
9g, Fat 7g, Fibre 1g, Sodium
300mg

Method

1. In a small or medium sauce pot, bring water to a boil and pour in rice. Reduce heat to low and cover. Allow to simmer for 50 minutes or until rice has absorbed all of the liquid. Once cooked, chill the rice.

2. In a medium bowl, mix carrot, yogurt, lime juice, salt, olive oil and curry powder. When all ingredients are combined, add drained tuna and break up with a fork.

3. Add tomatoes and cold rice and continue mixing.

4. Check seasoning and add pepper if desired.

5. Lay a desired amount of sprouts in centre of wrap and top with 2 heaping spoonfuls of rice mixture. Roll, and enjoy!

6. This can also be enjoyed as a salad without the wraps.

By choosing smaller fish, Raincoast Trading Albacore tuna is lower in mercury than other brands.

Bigoli and Tuna

Ingredients

8 tbsp	Omega Nutrition extra virgin olive oil
1	shallot, chopped
2	cloves garlic, chopped
15	Lindsay black olives, pitted and roughly chopped
100 ml	white wine (4 oz)
1	can Raincoast Trading Albacore tuna, drained (170 g)
1/2	lemon, juiced
1/4 tsp	chili flakes
1	small can plum tomatoes (396 ml)
1 tsp	oregano
500 g	Prairie Harvest whole wheat spaghetti or San Zenone gluten free pasta
2 tbsp	salt
	salt to taste
2 tbsp	chopped parsley

Serves 6

Nutrition Facts per Serving:
Calories 550, Carbohydrates 68g, Protein 21g, Fat 20g, Fibre 7g, Sodium 780mg

Method

1. In a frying pan, heat 4 tbsp of olive oil on medium heat and brown shallot and garlic.

2. Add olives and white wine.

3. Allow to reduce by half, then add tuna and lemon juice. Simmer for 5 minutes.

4. Stir in chili flakes and plum tomatoes, simmering for 15 more minutes.

5. Add oregano, mix well and check seasoning. If desired, add salt to taste.

6. Boil a large pot of water. Sprinkle in 2 tbsp salt and cook pasta.

7. When pasta is ready, drain and toss in a large bowl with sauce, remaining olive oil and fresh parsley.

Tofu Scaloppini

Ingredients

3 tbsp	Omega Nutrition extra virgin olive oil
1	small onion, sliced
2	green peppers, sliced
1 tbsp	fresh sage, chopped
3/4 cup	water
1	package Sunrise firm or extra firm tofu, sliced into 1/4 inch slices (350 g)
1 1/2	lemons, juiced
1 1/2 tbsp	tamari sauce, gluten free or regular
	black pepper to taste

Serves 4

Nutrition Facts per Serving:
Calories 220, Carbohydrates 8g, Protein 13g, Fat 16g, Fibre 2g, Sodium 360mg

Method

1. Over medium-high heat, heat oil in a large non-stick frying pan and brown onion.

2. When onion is golden, add green peppers, sautéing for 8 – 10 minutes or until peppers are softened.

3. Add 1/2 of the sage and 1/2 cup of water. When water has almost completely evaporated remove pepper mixture from frying pan.

4. Return frying pan to burner and brown tofu slices on both sides.

5. Add pepper mixture, remaining sage, lemon juice, tamari sauce and black pepper.

6. When liquid has partially evaporated, add remaining water then continue to cook until most liquid has evaporated.

Nutrition Tip: Eating more vegetarian protein is good for your heart and the planet!

Omega Rich Sweet Treats

Ingredients

1 cup	organic dried apricots, diced
1/2 cup	Omega Nutrition virgin coconut oil
2 tbsp	Camino Cuisine cocoa powder
2 tbsp	cocoa nibs
1 tsp	orange zest
3 tbsp	Mum's Original hemp seeds
2 tbsp	chia seeds

Serves 12

Nutrition Facts per Serving:
Calories 160, Carbohydrates 11g, Protein 3g, Fat 13g, Fibre 2g, Sodium 0mg

Method

1. In a food processor, blend apricots and coconut oil for about 30 seconds.

2. Add orange zest and cocoa powder, pulse for a few seconds.

3. Add cocoa nibs and hemp seeds, process until a ball starts to form.

4. Scoop mixture into the middle of a wax or parchment paper sheet. Fold paper over mixture and begin to roll slowly back and forth to form a cylinder about 6 or 7 inches long, about 1 to 1 1/2 inches in diameter.

5. Open paper and sprinkle part of the chia seeds on top, roll a bit further. Sprinkle the remainder of chia seeds on top and roll until all seeds have coated the outside of the roll.

6. Refrigerate, slice and serve.

Note: If you prefer, refrigerate the cylinder before coating with seeds then slice into 1/4 inch slices and roll into individual balls. Coat each individual ball with chia seeds or your favourite crushed nuts.

Nutrition Tip: these high energy treats are perfect for refueling during exercise but take care as they melt with body heat.

Chick Pea and Arugula Salad

Ingredients

1	can chick peas, drained and rinsed (390 ml)
1	medium tomato, diced
1	small red onion, diced
200 g	Happy Days goat feta, crumbled
1/2	lemon, juiced
2 tbsp	cilantro, chopped
3 tbsp	Omega Nutrition extra virgin olive oil
1 cup	fresh arugula, roughly chopped

Serves 5

Nutrition Facts per Serving:
Calories 300, Carbohydrates 16g, Protein 13g, Fat 21g, Fibre 4g, Sodium 310mg

Method

1. Combine all ingredients, leaving arugula for last.

2. Stir in arugula and serve immediately.

3. By leaving out arugula, salad can be made 24 hours ahead and store in fridge.

 *Nutrition Tip: Arugula is actually a cruciferous vegetable and contains a hefty dose of folate and potassium.*

Braised Brisket and Leeks

Ingredients

3	large leeks
1	small head of celery, chopped
1.7 kg	Diamond Willow organic brisket (3.5 – 4 lbs)
750 ml	red wine
1 tsp	salt
1 tsp	cracked black pepper
1/4 tsp	cinnamon
1/4 tsp	cloves
3 tbsp	Omega Nutrition extra virgin olive oil
1/2 L	beef stock

Serves 8

Nutrition Facts per Serving:
Calories (with sauce) 520,
Carbohydrates 12g, Protein
45g, Fat 24g, Fibre 1g,
Sodium 780mg

Method

1. Cut leeks in half and then slice each half in two, lengthwise. Slice each of the sections into small strips. Thoroughly wash leeks in cold water.

2. Season brisket with salt, pepper, cinnamon and cloves.

3. In heavy bottomed soup pot, heat olive oil on medium heat, browning brisket for 10 minutes on each side.

4. Reduce heat to medium-low, add celery and leeks. Cover.

5. Stir every 10 minutes to prevent sticking. If sticking occurs, reduce heat. After 30 minutes add wine.

6. Bring to a boil, reduce to simmer and cover for one hour.

7. Add stock. Bring to a boil again then reduce back to a simmer and cook covered for 3 more hours.

8. Remove brisket from sauce. Slice across the grain and serve with your favorite steamed grain, mashed potatoes or polenta.

Easy Coconut and Chicken Soup

Ingredients

1	Farmcrest specialty chicken breast (approximately 140 g), cubed
1	carrot
1	lime
1 tsp	freshly grated ginger
1 tbsp	lemon grass, grated
1 pinch	chili flakes
10 tsp	Gen Mai Miso
1 tbsp	sesame oil
1	can of coconut milk (400 ml)
4 cups	water
1/2	Napa cabbage

Serves 4

Nutrition Facts per Serving:
Calories 380, Carbohydrates 22g, Protein 15g, Fat 29g, Fibre 8g, Sodium 620mg

Method

1. In a heavy bottomed soup pot, warm the oil and cook the chicken.

2. Carrot can be sliced by hand, food processor or with the large blade on hand grater. Add sliced carrots to the cooking chicken.

3. Add miso and part of the water to make sure miso is dissolving. Add lime, ginger, lemon grass and chili flakes, water and bring to a boil.

4. Let simmer for a few moments and add coconut milk. Bring back to a boil and finish with shredded Napa cabbage.

Serve hot and garnish with sesame seeds if desired.

West Coast Potato Salad

Ingredients

2 lbs	medium red or white potatoes
1	red onion, chopped
250 g	hot smoked salmon, from Classic Smokehouse
1/4 cup	capers, chopped
150 g	cream cheese
2 tbsp	fresh sage, chopped
2 tbsp	Omega Nutrition apple cider vinegar
1/4 cup	Omega Nutrition extra virgin olive oil
1/2	lemon, juiced
2 tsp	paprika
1 tsp	sea salt
1/4 cup	water

Serves 8

Nutrition Facts per Serving:
Calories 340, Carbohydrate 41g, Protein 12g, Fat 15g, Fibre 6g, Sodium 720mg

Method

1. Boil potatoes whole, in abundant water until cooked but firm. Strain potatoes and allow to cool naturally (not in cold water). Once cool, cube potato into 3/4 inch cubes.

3. Cube salmon, making sure you remove all bones first.

4. Mix red onion, capers and sage in large bowl with cream cheese, apple cider vinegar, lemon juice, olive oil, paprika and salt.

5. Continue mixing until a uniform consistency is achieved. Add water and mix with potatoes and salmon. Eat immediately or refrigerate for up to 2 days in fridge.

Focus on Nutrition: Ever wonder about the cloudy matter at the bottom of apple cider vinegar? It is actually a probiotic!

Summer

Summer is a time of plenty – blue sky and sunlight bathes our soil and it is all about the show. Boastful ripe tomatoes, dark seductive cherries and plump cheerful berries return to delight our taste buds. As the weather heats up we turn to lighter foods that won't slow us down as we explore our beautiful province. Crunchy salads and cool juicy fruits will sustain us as the mercury rises. Now is the time when the die hard local eater becomes a busy bee, canning and freezing for the winter and the fair weather locavore simply relishes in seasonal riches. Explore all of the colours, shapes and textures of summer produce and create your own culinary magic! Take a long drive down a rural road and stop to pick your own berries or hop on your bike and get to know a farmer at a local market. Summer's delights only last a short time in our West Coast home so eat, drink and celebrate BC!

Fettuccine with Salmon and Fennel

Ingredients

500 g	fresh wild salmon from Classic Smokehouse, cubed
2 tbsp	Omega Nutrition extra virgin olive oil
1	small fennel bulb, cubed
8	sun dried tomatoes, chopped
1	lemon, juiced
500 ml	Dairyland whipping cream
1	pack Prairie Harvest Organic Egg Fettuccine or San Zenone Brown Rice Spaghetti (450 g)
1 g	saffron

Serves 6

Nutrition Facts per Serving:
Calories 700, Carbohydrate 64g, Protein 31g, Fat 37g, Fibre 4g, Sodium 160mg

Method

1. Heat olive oil in a large nonstick skillet on medium high heat and brown fennel.

2. Reduce heat to medium; add salmon and sundried tomatoes and cook for 6 – 8 minutes then add lemon juice.

3. Cook until lemon juice is absorbed and evaporated; next, add whipping cream and simmer.

4. In abundant, lightly salted boiling water, cook the egg noodles, approximately 8 – 10 minutes.

5. While noodles are cooking allow sauce to simmer gently; add saffron and salt to taste.

6. When pasta is fully cooked, strain and toss together with sauce. Serve immediately.

Focus on Nutrition: Saffron is the stigma of the saffron crocus, which must be picked by hand – each flower contains only 3 stigma!

Asian Salmon Curry

Ingredients

500 g	fresh wild salmon from Classic Smokehouse, cubed
2 tbsp +1 tbsp	Omega Nutrition virgin coconut oil
1	very large (or 2 medium) yellow onions, chopped
400 ml	coconut milk
150 g	mild curry paste
1	lime, juiced
1/2 cup	Olympic Organic 2% plain yogurt
2	large garlic cloves, chopped
1 tbsp	freshly grated ginger
1/2	cinnamon stick
1/2	bunch fresh cilantro
1/2 tsp	sea salt

Serves 4

Nutrition Facts per Serving:
Calories 520, Carbohydrate 12g, Protein 28g, Fat 42g, Fibre 4g, Sodium 270mg

Method

1. In a heavy bottomed saucepan on medium heat, heat 2 tbsp of virgin coconut oil. Sauté onion and garlic until translucent.

2. Add ginger, cloves, cinnamon and curry paste. Stir for 4 – 5 minutes.

3. Add lime juice and coconut milk and bring to a boil. Reduce to a simmer and add yogurt.

4. Heat 1 tbsp coconut oil in a skillet on medium high, then sauté salmon for 4 – 5 minutes. Sprinkle with salt and freshly chopped cilantro and transfer into saucepan.

5. Simmer for 5 more minutes and serve with steamed rice or your choice of grain.

Focus on Nutrition: Ginger is a potent anti-inflammatory spice and is traditionally used to ease nausea and tummy trouble.

Basic Vegetable Stock

Ingredients

2	carrots
1/2	stalk celery
1	onion, peeled
1	clove garlic, peeled
1/2	bunch parsley
1	turnip
1	bay leaf
5	peppercorns
1	red pepper
1	leek
8 L	water

Nutrition Facts per Serving:
Calories per cup (approximate)
15, Carbohydrates 3g,
Protein 0g, Fat 0g, Fibre 0g,
Sodium 20mg

Method

1. Place all ingredients in a large stock pot. Bring to a rapid boil then reduce to simmer for 2 hours.

2. Strain, reserving liquid. Refrigerate up to 4 or 5 days or freeze in desired portions for future use.

Summer Bean Salad

Ingredients

1.5 lb	yellow, green and purple beans
1	medium sweet onion, sliced
2 tbsp	Omega Nutrition balsamic vinegar
5 tbsp	Omega Nutrition extra virgin olive oil
1 tbsp	parsley, freshly chopped
1	clove garlic, chopped
	black pepper and salt to taste (optional)

Serves 4

Nutrition Facts per Serving:
Calories 210, Carbohydrate 15g, Protein 3g, Fat 17g, Fibre 6g, Sodium 10mg

Method

1. Clean beans then boil in abundant boiling water until tender crisp. Set aside to chill.

2. Once beans are chilled, combine all ingredients and mix well.

3. Allow to sit at room temperature for 30 minutes before serving. Use within 2 days.

Chilled Roasted Tomato Soup

Ingredients

9	medium field tomatoes
1 tbsp + 1/2 cup	Omega Nutrition Extra Virgin Olive Oil
1 tsp	sea salt
2	celery stalks
1	red pepper
2 tbsp	fresh basil, loosely chopped

Serves 4

Nutrition Facts per Serving:
Calories 340, Carbohydrate 13g, Protein 3g, Fat 33g, Fibre 4g, Sodium 420mg

Method

1. Preheat oven to 350° F.

2. Core tomatoes and cut in half. Toss tomatoes with 1/2 tsp salt and 1 tbsp olive oil. Bake, cut side up, for 1 hour 30 minutes. Allow tomatoes to completely cool.

3. Place red pepper, celery, 1/2 tsp sea salt and 1/2 cup olive oil in a food processor and process until smooth.

4. Add tomatoes and fresh basil and process until smooth.

5. Check seasoning and add more salt if desired.

Serve chilled with your choice of diced raw vegetables or tasty croutons. Use within 36 hours

Rosemary Chicken with Artichokes

Ingredients

8	large artichokes (or 12 small)
2 tbsp	fresh rosemary, finely chopped
3 tbsp	parsley, coarsely chopped
7 tbsp	Omega Nutrition extra virgin olive oil
2	lemons, juiced, plus an extra squeeze of lemon for lemon water
4	cloves garlic
4	Farmcrest specialty chicken breasts, boneless & skinless
1/2 cup	water (or low sodium chicken stock)
	sea salt to taste

Serves 4

Nutrition Facts per Serving:
Calories 490, Carbohydrate 9g, Protein 54g, Fat 27g, Fibre 3g, Sodium 190mg

Method

1. Trim artichokes, cut in half and remove all beard (fuzz). Place in bowl with water to cover and a squeeze of lemon juice or vinegar.

2. Heat oil in frying pan on medium high. Salt chicken and add to frying pan, outside of breast facing down. Brown for approximately 10 minutes.

3. Finely slice artichokes lengthwise, draining all excess water from each half. Add to frying pan.

4. Turn chicken and add to frying pan beside chicken: parsley, rosemary, 1 pinch of sea salt, and lemon juice; mix well.

5. Add 1/2 cup water or stock. Cover and simmer until most of the juices have evaporated, approximately 12 – 15 minutes, depending on the size of chicken breast.

Serve with steamed brown rice or whole grain of choice.

Jerk Chicken and Potato Salad

Ingredients

2	limes, juiced
2 tbsp	cilantro, chopped
1/4 cup	Jamaican jerk seasoning
1 kg	nugget potatoes
2 tbsp	Omega Nutrition extra virgin olive oil
2	green onions, finely chopped
1/2 tsp	sea salt
500 g	Farmcrest chicken breast, sliced

Serves 4

Nutrition Facts per Serving:
Calories 390, Carbohydrate 47g, Protein 31g, Fat 8g, Fibre 6g, Sodium 290mg

Method

1. Marinate chicken breast in a bowl with 1 tbsp cilantro and juice from 1 lime for a few hours or overnight if possible.

2. In a large frying pan, heat olive oil on high.

3. Cook chicken until fully cooked, about 7 – 10 minutes.

4. Chill all frying pan contents, including juices.

5. Boil whole nugget potatoes, drain and set aside to chill. Cube into 3/4 inch chunks once chilled.

6. Combine all remaining ingredients with chicken and potatoes.

Serve chilled or sauté and serve warm. Use within 3 days.

Focus on Nutrition: All members of the onion family contain diallyl sulfide, a phytochemical that helps protect against cancer.

Summer Bell Peppers
Stuffed with Eggplant Salad

Ingredients

1	large eggplant
2 cups	water
2 tbsp	red wine vinegar
8	small (or 4 large) multi-colored peppers (red, yellow, and orange)
4 tbsp	Omega Nutrition extra virgin olive oil
1	stalk celery, diced small
1	clove garlic, chopped
1	lemon, juiced
2 tbsp	fresh mint, chopped
1	green onion, finely chopped
1	tomato, diced small
3	pinches salt
	cracked pepper to taste

Serves 4 as an entree

Nutrition Facts per Serving:
Calories 200, Carbohydrate 20g, Protein 3g, Fat 14g, Fibre 8g, Sodium 135mg

Method

1. Preheat oven to 425° F. Pierce entire eggplant with fork and roast in oven for 25 minutes or until completely soft. Remove, cool, peel, and dice.

2. In a small pot, bring two cups of water to a boil with vinegar.

3. Insert peppers (if small, halved; if large, quartered) into boiling water and blanch for 40 seconds. Remove, drain, and place on baking sheet.

4. In a frying pan, heat oil on medium-high heat and brown celery.

5. Add garlic, diced eggplant and salt. Sauté for 4 – 5 minutes and add lemon juice, mint, green onion and tomatoes.

6. Remove from heat and fill peppers with spoonfuls of the eggplant mixture.

7. Return to oven for 15 minutes. Serve hot or cold.

Variation

Half a cup of crumbled feta or parmesan may be added to mixture if desired. Recipe can also serve 8 as an appetizer

Focus on Nutrition:
Eggplant contains soluble fibre,
which helps to lower cholesterol.

Gingered Fruit Salad

Ingredients

1	small cantaloupe or 1/2 large
1	small honeydew or 1/2 large
4	kiwis
1/2 cup	Luc Bergeron Organic maple syrup
1 tbsp	ginger, freshly grated
1	lemon, juiced

Serves 6

Nutrition Facts per Serving:
Calories 190, Carbohydrate 47g, Protein 2g, Fat 0.5g, Fibre 4g, Sodium 45mg

Method

1. Cut all fruit into 1 inch cubes. If preferred, melon can be scooped using a melon baller. Peel kiwi and quarter before slicing.

2. Mix maple syrup, ginger and lemon together then pour over fruit.

3. Allow to chill for at least 12 hours in the fridge before serving and use within 48 hours.

Swiss Steak of Salmon with Radish Salad

Ingredients

400 g	salmon, from Classic Smokehouse
2 tbsp	brown sugar
1 tbsp + 1 tsp	salt
1 oz	gin
1/2	lemon, rind only, chopped
3	green onions, chopped
6	Lindsay medium pitted olives, chopped
1	small shallot, chopped
1/2	celery stalk, chopped
1 tsp	ground black pepper
1 tbsp	fresh rosemary, chopped
1 tbsp	Dijon mustard
3 tbsp	Omega Nutrition extra virgin olive oil
1 cup	cherry tomatoes, quartered
1	lemon
1	bunch radishes, quartered
1	carrot, diced
2 tbsp	flat leaf parsley, freshly chopped

Serves 6 as an appetizer

Nutrition Facts per Serving:
Calories 220, Carbohydrate 13g, Protein 15g, Fat 12g, Fibre 3g, Sodium 1390mg

Method

1. Sprinkle brown sugar and 1 tbsp salt over salmon. Rest in fridge for at least 2 – 3 hours then rinse under cold water and pat dry.

2. Skin and chop salmon. Add shallot, celery, lemon rind, olives and rosemary to salmon.

3. Add lemon juice, ground pepper, Dijon mustard, gin and mix. Refrigerate for at least 30 minutes.

4. Form 6 small, thick patties, about 2 inches wide and 1 inch thick.

5. Heat 2 tbsp of olive oil in heavy bottomed non-stick skillet and brown patties on each side.

6. Place cherry tomatoes, radishes, green onions, parsley and carrot into a bowl and dress with 1 tbsp olive oil and 1 tbsp lemon juice and a pinch of salt.

Serve each patty with a scoop of salad.

Focus on Nutrition: In addition to their high omega 3 content, salmon is also the richest food source of vitamin D – the sunshine vitamin!

Tunisian Salad

Ingredients

1	large fennel bulb (or 2 small)
1	bunch radishes, sliced
1/2	bunch Italian parsley, coarsely chopped
3	small carrots, sliced
4	green onions, chopped
1/2 cup	Lindsay black olives
2 cups	cherry tomatoes, halved
1 1/2	lemons, juiced
4 tbsp	Omega Nutrition extra virgin olive oil
1 tsp	sea salt
4	hard boiled eggs (optional)

Serves 4

Nutrition Facts per Serving:
Calories (with egg) 280,
Carbohydrates 20g, Protein
10g, Fat 20g, Fibre 7g,
Sodium 580mg

Method

1. Discard top of fennel and slice fennel bulb.

2. Combine lemon juice, salt and oil.

3. Toss all ingredients in large bowl with dressing and chill for 1/2 hour.

4. Serve with a sliced boiled egg (optional).

 *Focus on Nutrition: Fennel is considered a cooling food in Ayurveda, the traditional Indian system of medicine.*

Pasta with Raw Tomato Sauce

Ingredients

12	fresh Roma tomatoes (or 8 medium field tomatoes)
5 tbsp	Omega Nutrition extra virgin olive oil
4	cloves garlic
2	small bunches basil (or flat leaf parsley)
	sea salt to taste (optional)
1	package Prairie Harvest Organic Whole Wheat Spaghetti or San Zenone Brown Rice Penne (454 g)

Serves 6

Nutrition Facts per Serving:
Calories 430, Carbohydrate 66g, Protein 14g, Fat 13g, Fibre 9g, Sodium 10mg

Method

1. Wash and core tomatoes, squeezing excess seeds and juice into sink.

2. Put olive oil and garlic in blender. Blend together, adding one tomato at a time until completely pureed.

3. Add rough chopped basil and salt (optional), puree until combined.

4. Mix with cooked pasta.

Focus on Nutrition: Famous for their lycopene content, raw tomatoes also boast chlorogenic acid which helps to inhibit environmental toxins like nitrosamines in our bodies.

Salmon Stuffed Chicken Breast with Celery Salsa

Ingredients

3	Farmcrest specialty chicken breasts, boneless skinless, approx 600 g total
100 g	fresh wild salmon, from Classic Smokehouse
110 g	Happy Days goat cheese
2	sundried tomatoes
1 tbsp	fresh tarragon, chopped
1	organic lemon, juiced and zested
4 tbsp	capers, chopped
1	stalk celery, small diced
1/2	red onion, finely diced
2 tbsp	Omega Nutrition cold pressed High – O sunflower seed oil
2 tbsp	Omega Nutrition extra virgin olive oil
1/4 tsp	fresh ground black pepper
3 pinches	salt

Serves 3

Nutrition Facts per Serving:
Calories 580, Carbohydrate 15g, Protein 60g, Fat 31g, Fibre 4g, Sodium 840mg

Method

1. Preheat oven to 430° F.

2. Soak 2 sundried tomatoes in 1/2 cup hot water for 30 minutes. Drain and cool.

2. In food processor, add roughly chopped salmon, chopped tarragon, goat cheese, sun dried tomatoes, 1 tbsp lemon juice, 1/4 tsp lemon zest and process until smooth.

3. Insert a small sharp knife into the thicker end of each breast, making an incision through 2/3 of the breast, forming an internal pocket. Take care not to cut open at the sides.

4. With piping bag, stuff salmon goat cheese mixture equally between chicken breasts.

5. Heat olive oil in oven friendly frying pan. Brown "skinless skin side" first and once flipped bake for 20 minutes.

6. Combine celery, onion and capers with lemon juice and sunflower seed oil in a small bowl.

Serve chicken hot or cold with the Celery Salsa.

Salmon and Watercress Salad

Ingredients

1 1/2 cups	dry organic french green lentils, presoaked (at least 6 hours)
300 g	wild salmon fillet, from Classic Smokehouse
1/2	orange, zest only
1/2	lemon, zest only
1	lime, juiced + zest from half the fruit
1 tbsp	fresh ginger, grated
5 tbsp	Omega Nutrition extra virgin olive oil
2 cups	watercress, tips and leaves, washed and drained

Serves 4

Nutrition Facts per Serving:
Calories 550, Carbohydrate 38g, Protein 37g, Fat 23g, Fibre 27g, Sodium 45mg

Method

1. After discarding the soaking water, cook lentils in abundant water until tender, approximately 35 minutes. When soft, remove, strain and set aside.

2. Preheat oven to 375° F.

3. Place salmon, skin down, on a small baking sheet. Sprinkle with lime, lemon and orange zest, and sea salt (optional). Bake for 18 – 20 minutes.

4. Combine lime juice, olive oil, ginger and salt to taste (optional). Mix dressing with lentils (cold or hot).

5. Remove salmon from skin, cube it and mix with lentils. Add watercress immediately prior to serving.

 *Focus on Nutrition: Lentils are high in protein, fibre and contain plant sterols to help lower blood cholesterol.*

Harvest Cherry Crumble

Ingredients

2 lbs	large cherries
1/2 +1/2 cup	brown sugar
3 tsp	corn starch
1	lime, juice
1	lemon, juiced + zested
1 1/2 tsp	ginger, grated
1/3 cup	Omega Nutrition virgin coconut oil
4 cups	gluten free cereal flakes
1/8 tsp	ground cinnamon

Serves 8

Nutrition Facts per Serving:
Calories 310, Carbohydrates 60g, Protein 2g, Fat 9g, Fibre 3g, Sodium 110mg

Method

1. Preheat oven to 350° F.

2. Wash and pit all cherries – if smaller cherries are being used, use more than 2 pounds worth.

3. Mix cherries with 1/2 cup brown sugar, juice of lemon and lime, ginger and cinnamon. Sprinkle with corn starch and mix well.

4. Pour mixture into 7 inch x 7 inch (20cm x 20cm) Pyrex.

5. Mix coconut oil, remaining sugar, lemon zest and cereal – making sure to "crumble" all of the flakes. Top the cherries with this crumble mixture and bake for 1 hour and 20 minutes.

Enjoy warm or at room temperature on its own or with your favourite ice cream!

 *Focus on Nutrition: Tart local cherries are one of nature's only food sources of melatonin, a natural sleep inducing antioxidant.*

Radicchio, Fig and Orange Salad

Ingredients

1	firm head of radicchio
1 large	navel orange
5 tbsp	Olympic Organic 2% plain yogurt
4 tbsp	chopped dried figs
2 1/2 tbsp	gomashio (sesame salt)
1 1/2 tbsp	Omega Nutrition apple cider vinegar
4 tbsp	crushed almonds

Serves 4

Nutrition Facts per Serving:
Calories 210, Carbohydrate 20g, Protein 7g, Fat 12g, Fibre 6g, Sodium 370mg

Method

1. Slice, wash and dry radicchio. With a small serrated knife, remove peel and pith from the orange, leaving only clean orange segments, then dice.

3. Combine all ingredients except radicchio in a large bowl and mix vigorously and then toss in the radicchio.

Focus on Nutrition: Yogurt has been considered a health food for centuries...rich in calcium and protein, the probiotic cultures in yogurt also help maintain digestive health.

Vegetable Ripieni

Ingredients

3	small zucchini
3	small peppers - yellow, red, orange
1	small yellow onion, finely chopped
2	cloves garlic, finely chopped
2	egg whites
1 tbsp	dried oregano
2 tbsp	flat leaf parsley, chopped
2 pinches	cinnamon
1 cup	grated parmesan
2 tsp +1/4 tsp	sea salt
1 1/2 cups	French bread
1 1/4 cup	Dairyland Organic 2% milk
2 +1 tbsp	Omega Nutrition extra virgin olive oil
1/4 tsp	freshly ground black pepper

**Serves 8 as appetizers
(3 pieces each)**

Nutrition Facts per Serving:
Calories 320, Carbohydrate 37g, Protein 18g, Fat 12g, Fibre 4g, Sodium 930mg

Method

1. Preheat oven to 450° F.

2. Cut zucchini lengthwise and then in half. With a small teaspoon, scoop out pulp, turning quarter zucchinis into little canoes. Cut peppers in quarters, lengthwise.

3. Boil approximately 4 litres of water with 2 tsp sea salt and blanch zucchini and peppers for about 90 seconds. Set aside.

4. In a large frying pan, brown onions, garlic and zucchini pulp for about 7 – 10 minutes.

4. Add oregano, cinnamon, chopped parsley, black pepper and 1/4 tsp salt.

5. Soak bread in milk, working with your hands until bread has absorbed all liquid. Add to cooking vegetable mixture and cook for 5 more minutes. Remove and chill.

6. Whip egg whites. Combine bread and veggie mix with egg whites and pipe with bag or spoon into blanched vegetables.

7. Bake for 15 minutes. Serve hot or cold.

Pork Tenderloin with Apricots

Ingredients

450 g	pork tenderloin
1/2 tsp	cinnamon
2 tsp	black pepper, coarsely ground
1 tsp	sea salt
2 tbsp	Omega Nutrition extra virgin olive oil
8	apricots, cut in wedges
2 tbsp	brown sugar
1 tsp	fresh ginger, grated
1/2	lemon, juiced
2 tsp	fresh thyme, chopped

Serves 4

Nutrition Facts per Serving:
Calories 260, Carbohydrate
16g, Protein 25g, Fat 11g,
Fibre 2g, Sodium 450mg

Method

1. Sprinkle cinnamon, ground pepper and salt on the tenderloin.

2. In a frying pan, heat oil and brown seasoned whole pork tenderloin on both sides.

3. Remove pork from frying pan. To pan, add apricot wedges, sugar, ginger, cook for 2 – 3 minutes and add lemon juice and thyme.

4. Return tenderloin back to pan, reduce heat and add 2 tbsp water. Cover and simmer each side for 7 – 8 minutes.

5. Turn off and allow to stand covered for 10 – 15 minutes prior to slicing.

Sunny Slopes Farm
Naramata BC

It is now more than twenty years since Friedrich and Marianne Keim came to the Okanagan from Nuremberg, Germany to escape the devastating pollution that Chernobyl left behind. To them it was Paradise and they set about to create their own Garden of Eden buying a soft-fruit farm on the sunny slopes of the Naramata bench. Prior to the Keims' arrival, the farm had been conventionally managed with sprays and chemical fertilizer and they were determined to make changes. Sunny Slopes Farm became a BC certified organic farm, where the trees were nourished with compost and minerals and pest management was done by hand. The Keims' experience in biodynamic farming in Germany prepared them well for the challenges of organic farming.

With such an organic bounty, the Keim Family now struggled with how to market their luscious fruit. With wholesalers and mass retailers being such a long distance, fruit would have to be picked too early. Never content to let the true beauty of their peaches go unnoticed, Sunny Slopes decided to bring their wares directly to the market and they found us here at Choices Markets. Under the guidance of our produce guru, David Wilson, a direct marketing approach was reached that allowed the gorgeous peaches to fully ripen in their trees.

To reach our customers, peaches are picked early morning, packed in a single layer so as not to damage them and land in our produce department the very next day. This exquisite fruit is bursting with ripe juicy flavour and is just waiting for you to come and take them home!

Mustard Crusted Salmon

Ingredients

700 g	wild salmon fillet, from Classic Smokehouse
3 tbsp	brown sugar
3 tbsp	coarse sea salt
130 g	french bread, cubed
2 tbsp	Omega Nutrition virgin coconut oil
1/2 tsp	sea salt
30 g	green onions or chives, roughly chopped
2 1/2 tbsp	prepared mustard

Serves 4

Nutrition Facts per Serving:
Calories 480, Carbohydrate 32g, Protein 42g, Fat 22g, Fibre 3g, Sodium 1950mg

Method

1. Sprinkle salt and sugar on salmon fillet and let sit in fridge for 3 hours. Rinse in cold water and pat dry.

2. Preheat oven to 375°F.

3. In food processor, combine bread, coconut oil, sea salt and green onions. Process until uniform and crumbly.

4. Spread mustard evenly on one side of the fish and distribute the bread mixture over top of the fish.

5. Bake for 25 minutes – dish can be made as one fillet or as 4 individual pieces.

Serve with fresh fennel salad or other salad of choice. Enjoy!

Focus on Nutrition: The gorgeous pink colour of salmon comes from astaxanthin, a potent anti-oxidant.

Mediterranean Pearl Salad

Ingredients

6	medium tomatoes, cored and cut into large cubes
1	bunch Basil, washed, roughly chopped
1	small can artichoke hearts packed in water, drained and quartered
200 g	bocconcini pearls, or chopped bocconcini
1	head fresh garlic
1	lemon, zested and juiced
3 tbsp	Omega Nutrition extra virgin olive oil
1 1/2	Omega Nutrition balsamic vinegar
1 1/2	black olive paste or tapenade
	sea salt to taste

Serves 4

Nutrition Facts per Serving:
Calories 340, Carbohydrates 19g, Protein 15g, Fat 26g, Fibre 7g, Sodium 290mg

Method

1. Cut top off head of garlic, lightly brush with olive oil, wrap in foil and bake for 25 minutes at 375° F.

2. Allow garlic to cool a bit, squeeze out of peel and mash with lemon juice, olive oil, balsamic vinegar, black olive paste and sea salt to make dressing.

3. Combine with remaining ingredients in large bowl and serve.

Turkey and Shiitake Summer Stew

Ingredients

3 tbsp	Omega Nutrition extra virgin olive oil
2	extra large garlic cloves, sliced
7 or 8	red and yellow peppers, sliced
1 cup	Shiitake mushrooms, sliced
2 tbsp	fresh marjoram
850 g	JD Farms specialty turkey breast, boneless, skinless, cubed
1/4 cup	corn starch
2 cups	chicken stock
2	lemons, juiced
1 tbsp	Omega Nutrition balsamic vinegar
1/2 tbsp	sea salt
	pepper to taste

Serves 8

Nutrition Facts per Serving:
Calories 620, Carbohydrate 21g, Protein 31g, Fat 9g, Fibre 2g, Sodium 430mg

---

Method

1. In a large skillet or wok heat 1 tbsp of olive oil. Sauté garlic and sliced peppers until they start to caramelize but are still crisp. Remove peppers from skillet and set aside.

2. Sauté mushrooms in 1 tbsp of olive oil. Lightly salt the mushrooms with part of the sea salt. Prior to removing from the skillet, add half of the marjoram and set aside.

3. Deglaze skillet with 1/2 of the stock and pour over vegetables.

4. Heat the remaining olive oil. Season turkey cubes with remaining sea salt. Coat in corn starch and place in pan to sear. When turkey is completely seared, add remaining chicken stock and lemon juice.

5. Return all vegetables to the skillet. Add balsamic vinegar; simmer until all juices have reduced to stew-like consistently.

Serve with your favorite grain - couscous, rice, potato, millet, bread, or polenta

Focus on Nutrition: Turkey breast is a lean source of protein and is low in saturated fat – making it a heart healthy choice.

Pasta Alla Caprese

Ingredients

12	ripe roma tomatoes (or canned San Marzano tomatoes out of season)
2	cloves of garlic
1/2 cup	Omega Nutrition extra virgin olive oil
1/2 tsp	sea salt + approx 2 tbsp for pasta water
450 g	Prairie Harvest or San Zenone short pasta – rigatoni, farfalle, or penne (1 package)
1	handful fresh basil leaves, roughly chopped
1 cup	bocconcini pearls (or cubed regular bocconcini)

Serves 6

Nutrition Facts per Serving:
Calories 530, Carbohydrates 61g, Protein 16g, Fat 26g, Fibre 4g, Sodium 300mg

Method

1. Core tomatoes with an X on the tip and squeeze out excess seeds and water.

2. Put garlic and oil into a food processor and process; add tomatoes and salt, and continue to process.

3. Add basil and finish processing.

4. Cook pasta in abundant water until "al dente" and strain. Mix first with the bocconcini and then mix in tomato sauce. Serve immediately.

This dish can also be used to create a delicious pasta salad! Just chill the pasta before mixing all ingredients and refrigerate.

Summer Peach and Coconut Soup

Ingredients

4	large peaches
1/2	lemon, juiced
400 ml	coconut milk
1 cup	orange juice
1 tbsp	rosemary, freshly chopped or lavender flowers
1 pinch	sea salt
	ground black pepper to taste

Serves 4

Nutrition Facts per Serving:
Calories 330, Carbohydrate 28g, Protein 4g, Fat 25g, Fibre 5g, Sodium 115mg

Method

1. Peel peaches and place all ingredients in food processor for 3 – 4 minutes and process until smooth.

2. Refrigerate for a few hours and enjoy. Use within 48 hours.

Note: If skin is hard to remove which may happen if peach is not fully ripe, score peach with a cross on the opposite side of the peach stem. Bring a few litres of water to a boil and introduce 1 peach at a time for 40 to 60 seconds, remove and place in an ice bath in order to remove skin.

Focus on Nutrition: Coconut contains lauric acid, a fatty acid which is currently being studied for its potential immune benefits.

Fall

From the dog days of summer, the cool air and clear sunshine of autumn offer a welcome reprieve. Happy school children bumping down the road bring visions of crisp red apples and freshly sharpened pencils. Crates of fresh apples, pears and cranberries blend into the golden and burnished hues of the changing leaves. Fall is a time of return: to routine, to introspection, to a slower pace. Stir some local honey into a cup of tea and enjoy the cool autumn evenings; hunt for a perfectly scary jack o' lantern in a local pumpkin patch. Fill your kitchen with the perfume of baking pies; crush some quince paste and invite friends over for an evening of wine and cheese and recall the frivolities of summer.

Millet and Romaine Wraps

Ingredients

1/2 cup	millet
2 cups	water
1	can white navy beans or your favorite beans, washed and drained (398 ml)
1 tbsp	curry powder
1 tbsp	Omega Nutrition apple cider vinegar
1 tsp	sea salt
1/2 cup	Olympic Organic 2% plain yogurt
1/2 cup	carrots, shredded
4	green onions, chopped
1	large head of romaine

Serves 6

Nutrition Facts per Serving:
Calories 290, Carbohydrate 53g, Protein 16g, Fat 2g, Fibre 18g, Sodium 280mg

Method

1. Wash millet and bring to a boil in 2 cups water; reduce to simmer for approximately 35 minutes, covered. Remove from heat and allow to cool.

2. Mash the beans with back of a spoon in a large bowl. Combine with curry powder, apple cider, salt and yogurt. Add millet.

3. Wash all larger leaves of romaine, trying not to tear them.

4. Remove a triangular shape (approx 2 inches in length) of the crunchiest part of the stalk from the base of each leaf. Finely shred the stalks with a knife and reserve for later use.

5. Place two leaves on top of each other, with cut bases at opposite ends.

6. Spoon about 3 tbsp of millet mixture in the centre of the leaves. Add 1 tbsp of shredded carrot, then some shredded lettuce stalk, about "two leaves" worth. Roll, folding outside edges in first. Serve whole or cut on the bias.

 *Focus on Nutrition: An ancient grain common in African cuisines, millet is gluten free and higher in iron and copper than brown rice.*

Smoked Herring and Heritage Grains Salad

Ingredients

1/2 cup	wild rice
1/2 cup	quinoa
1/2 cup	carrots, grated
1	lemon, juiced
3	green onions, finely chopped
2 tbsp	Italian parsley, finely chopped
4 tbsp	Omega Nutrition extra virgin olive oil
1/2 tsp	sea salt
2	cans (190 g) smoked herrings, from Classic Smokehouse

Serves 4

Nutrition Facts per Serving:
Calories 380, Carbohydrate 32g, Protein 17g, Fat 21g, Fibre 3g, Sodium 270mg

Method

1. Bring 2 cups of water to a boil and cook wild rice, simmering until tender, about 30 minutes. Drain and set aside.

2. Bring 1 cup of water to a boil and cook quinoa, covered and simmering for about 12 minutes. Set aside to cool.

3. Drain fish from water and mix with all other ingredients into chilled grains.

4. Chill before serving and use within 3 days.

Focus on Nutrition: Herring, like all oily fish, are a source of heart healthy omega 3 fatty acids.

Vatellina Style Cabbage Rolls

Ingredients

1	medium head savoy cabbage
1 tbsp +1 tsp	sea salt
4 tbsp	red wine vinegar
1/2 cup	butter, unsalted,organic
1	large Sweet onion, sliced
1/3 cup	millet (uncooked)
1 1/3 cup	water
10	shallots
2 tbsp	Omega Nutrition extra virgin olive oil
1	package fresh sage (14 g)
1 tbsp	coarse black pepper
300 g	cave aged Gruyere (or substitute favourite cheese)

Serves 6

Nutrition Facts per Serving:
Calories 530, Carbohydrate 37g, Protein 22g, Fat 37g, Fibre 6g, Sodium 610mg

Method

1. Preheat oven to 375° F.

2. Peel off outer leaves of cabbage. Discard any rough, fibrous leaves. Take the first 8 – 12 larger leaves and blanch in boiling vinegar water with sea salt for 7 – 8 minutes. Remove and set aside.

3. Shred remaining cabbage. In a heavy bottomed sauce pan, heat 1/4 cup butter until it starts to brown. Add 2 cups of shredded cabbage and stew for approximately 10 minutes, stirring constantly.

4. Add onion and stew 15 minutes, stirring.

5. Add millet and water and bring to a boil. Reduce heat to simmer, covered, until all liquid has been absorbed. Set mixture aside.

6. Peel shallots and roast in olive oil in oven until golden brown.

7. Roughly chop roasted shallots and fresh sage, and combine with millet cabbage stew and pepper.

8. Cut cheese into sticks (approximately 2 inches long).

9. Cut out stem at the base of each blanched cabbage leaf to make leaf easier to roll. Place one cheese stick and approx 3 heaping tablespoons of millet cabbage stew across the top of the leaf. Fold sides in, and roll up leave tightly. Place in Pyrex baking dish. Repeat with all leaves. Bake for 20 minutes.

10. Prior to serving, brown remaining butter and pour over top of cabbage rolls.

Greek Style
Wilted Mustard Greens

Ingredients

1	bunch chard, loosely chopped
1	bunch mustard greens, loosely chopped
1	large red onion, sliced
2	garlic cloves, minced
75 ml	Omega Nutrition extra virgin olive oil
3/4 cup	Happy Days goat feta, crumbled
1 tsp	dried oregano
2	lemons, juiced
1 tbsp	Omega Nutrition balsamic vinegar

Serves 6

Nutrition Facts per Serving:
Calories 240, Carbohydrate 14g, Protein 6g, Fat 20g, Fibre 6g, Sodium 430mg

Method

1. In a large frying pan, heat oil on medium heat and sauté sliced red onion.

2. When starting to brown, add garlic, loosely chopped chard and greens. Stir constantly for about 7 – 10 minutes then add lemon juice and dried oregano and allow to evaporate while stirring.

3. Add balsamic vinegar and crumbled feta. Mix and serve warm as a side dish.

Variation

If desired, before adding lemon juice you could add 1 1/2 ounces of Ouzo or Sambuca and allow to evaporate prior to adding the lemon juice.

Focus on Nutrition: Bitter greens contain sulphur compounds which help to detoxify the body.

Green Lentil, Kale and Spinach Soup

Ingredients

1	bunch fresh spinach, chopped
1	bunch black lacinato kale, chopped
1 cup	green lentils, soaked for 12 hours and drained
2	cloves garlic, chopped
3	Omega Nutrition extra virgin olive oil
3 tbsp	Omega Nutrition extra virgin olive oil
1 tbsp	parsley, chopped
	salt and pepper to taste
1 1/2 L	chicken stock (or your favorite stock)

Serves 6

Nutrition Facts per Serving:
Calories 330, Carbohydrate 32g, Protein 18g, Fat 16g, Fibre 14g, Sodium 820mg

Method

1. In a heavy saucepan, heat 3 tbsp olive oil. Sweat onion and garlic. When translucent, add spinach and continue stewing.

2. When spinach is completely wilted, add kale, lentils and stock.

3. Bring to a boil and simmer for at least 45 minutes or until lentils are tender. Season just before removing from stove. Add remaining olive oil and parsley.

Lentil Coconut Soup

Ingredients

1	onion, chopped
3	stalks celery, diced
2	large apples, cubed
3	cloves garlic
3 tbsp	Omega Nutrition virgin coconut oil
2 cups	organic red lentils
2 tbsp	curry powder
1	can coconut milk (400 ml)
6 1/2 cups	vegetable stock or water
1	lime, juiced
	sea salt to taste (optional)

Serves 8

Nutrition Facts per Serving:
Calories 400, Carbohydrate 48g, Protein 16g, Fat 19g, Fibre 10g, Sodium 30mg

Method

1. In a heavy bottomed soup pot, sweat onion, garlic and celery in coconut oil on medium heat for approximately 15 minutes, stirring constantly.

2. Add apples and sweat for another 10 minutes, stirring constantly.

3. Stir in curry powder and 1/2 cup water or stock and continue cooking for another 10 minutes, stirring.

4. Add lentils and remaining liquid and bring to a boil, stirring. Simmer 20 minutes.

5. Once lentils are fully cooked, add coconut milk.

6. Liquefy with an emersion blender (hand held). Add lime juice. Salt to taste.

Sprouted Red Wheat Tabouleh

Ingredients

1 cup	red wheat
1/4	white onion, finely chopped
3 tbsp	fresh mint, chopped
1/2 cup	flat leaf parsley, chopped
1	lemon, juiced
1/2 tsp	sea salt
2	green onions, finely chopped
3 tbsp	Omega Nutrition extra virgin olive oil

Serves 6

Nutrition Facts per Serving:
Calories 170, Carbohydrate 24g, Protein 5g, Fat 7g, Fibre 5g, Sodium 170mg

Method

1. Soak wheat with 3 cups of cold water for 24 hours in the fridge. Strain and lightly rinse.

2. Place in glass Pyrex dish while still moist and cover with cheese cloth or plastic wrap with a few air holes cut in. Leave in a bright spot (not direct sunlight) for at least 72 hours (sprouting might be slower or faster due to different environmental conditions: light, temperature, etc).

3. Rinse sprouts and drain.

4. Place in a bowl and mix with all ingredients and eat immediately.

When sprouting grains, keep all ingredients and utensils extremely clean. Those with weakened immune systems should avoid eating home-sprouted food.

Clover and Cucumber Salad

Ingredients

1 tsp	salt
5 tbsp	Happy Days plain goat yogurt
2	tomatoes
1	cucumber
1	container clover sprouts
1	container onion sprouts
1	container broccoli sprouts

Serves 6 as an appetizer or side dish

Nutrition Facts per Serving:
Calories 15, Carbohydrate 3g, Protein 1g, Fat 0g, Fibre 1g, Sodium 390mg

Method

1. Cube tomatoes and cucumber into small pieces.

2. Mix together with goat yogurt and salt.

3. Line 6 individual plates with mixture of sprouts and top with a dollop of tomato/cucumber mixture.

Focus on Nutrition:
Broccoli sprouts contain more sulphoraphane, the cancer fighting phytochemical, than mature broccoli.

Granny Smith and Zola Salad

Ingredients

50 g	gorgonzola
1/4 cup	Dairyland whipping cream
2 tsp	Omega Nutrition apple cider vinegar
2	Granny Smith apples, diced
1/2	celery stalk, small diced
1 tsp	cracked black pepper
1/4 tsp	sea salt
2	heads Belgian endive

Serves 4

Nutrition Facts per Serving:
Calories 170, Carbohydrate 19g, Protein 6g, Fat 9g, Fibre 10g, Sodium 260mg

Method

1. In a bowl combine cheese, whipping cream, salt and pepper and mash with a spoon until all ingredients are combined.

2. Toss in apple and celery, add apple cider vinegar and mix again.

3. Cut Belgian endive in small strips lengthwise, and add to salad. Mix and enjoy!

Potato and Artichoke Tart

Ingredients

2 lbs	russet potatoes (approx 3 large + 2 medium)
3	large artichokes, trimmed and sliced
4	cloves garlic, sliced
3 tbsp	butter
4 tbsp	fresh flat leaf parsley, chopped
3 tbsp	Omega Nutrition extra virgin olive oil
1	lemon, juiced
1/2 cup	white wine
1/2 tsp	salt
3	large eggs
1 cup	Dairyland Organic 2% milk

Serves 6

Nutrition Facts per Serving:
Calories 350, Carbohydrate 39g, Protein 11g, Fat 16g, Fibre 8g, Sodium 330mg

Method

1. Peel potatoes. Cube the 3 large potatoes and cook in abundant water until soft. Strain and mash with butter. Cool to room temperature.

2. Preheat oven to 350° F.

3. Line 8 x 8 baking dish with the mashed potatoes by spreading the mash evenly along the bottom and up the sides, forming a shell. Bake the potato shell at 350° F for 30 minutes or until shell feels dry to touch. Preheat oven to 375° F.

4. In a skillet, heat olive oil on medium heat and add garlic cloves, 2 tbsp parsley and artichokes. Continue cooking on medium heat for 10 – 15 minutes.

5. Add lemon juice and white wine and cook to reduce liquid by half. Add 2 medium potatoes, cut in 1 inch x 1/4 inch strips. Cook until all liquid is absorbed. Add salt.

6. In a bowl, mix eggs, 2 tbsp chopped parsley and milk. Remove artichoke mixture from stove and pour into baked potato shell, patting it lightly to even out. Pour egg mixture over top. Bake for 40 minutes.

Roasted Local Chicken and Veggies

Ingredients

1	medium Farmcrest Specialty chicken (approx 2.5 – 3 lbs) cut in 8 pieces (or 8 thighs, 8 drumsticks, or 4 large breasts)
2 tbsp	Omega Nutrition extra virgin olive oil
3	cloves garlic, minced
3	medium Yukon gold potatoes, cubed, skin on
2	red or yellow peppers cut in strips
2	green peppers cut in strips
1 cup	red wine
1/4 tbsp	sea salt
	fresh oregano sprig
	coarse black pepper

Serves 4

Nutrition Facts per Serving:
Calories 490, Carbohydrate 38g, Protein 38g, Fat 16g, Fibre 6g, Sodium 590mg

Method

1. Preheat oven to 410° F.

2. Heat oil in large skillet and place chicken pieces, skin down, browning very well.

3. Add potatoes and garlic and continue cooking and stirring until chicken skin is completely golden.

4. Add peppers and continue stirring. Add fresh oregano sprig whole.

5. Place chicken and veggies on a baking dish.

6. Deglaze skillet with 1 cup red wine and pour onto chicken mixture. Bake for 35 minutes, stirring every 10 – 15 minutes.

Focus on Nutrition:
Don't underestimate the health benefits of herbs – oregano has an antioxidant ORAC value of almost 14000 vs 6500 for blueberries!

Maple Salmon Croutons with Roasted Tomato Salsa

Ingredients

4	medium tomatoes (or 6 – 7 Romas)
200 g	Happy Days goat cheese
150 g	maple salmon nuggets from Classic Smokehouse
2 tbsp	chopped fresh tarragon (divided in two)
1	lemon, zested and juiced
1 tbsp	Omega Nutrition extra virgin olive oil
1 tsp	salt
1	baguette
	Black pepper to taste

Serves 8 as an appetizer

Nutrition Facts per Serving:
Calories 280, Carbohydrate 34g, Protein 15g, Fat 10g, Fibre 3g, Sodium 760mg

Method

1. Preheat oven to 375° F.

2. Cut 3 tomatoes in half and bake for 1.5 hours.

3. In a food processor, process goat cheese, lemon zest, maple nuggets, 1 tbsp of chopped tarragon and 1/2 the lemon juice until smooth.

4. Cube the remaining raw tomato and the roasted tomatoes and combine in a bowl with remaining lemon juice, chopped tarragon, salt, and oil.

5. Serve on your favorite baguette, sliced on a bias. Spread cheese salmon mixture first, and top with an abundant teaspoon of salsa.

Mojito Chutney

Ingredients

1 lb	organic sweet limes, diced, skin on
200 g	organic onions, chopped
50 g	organic carrots, diced
10 g	mint, chopped
100 g	Cuisine Camino organic golden sugar
100 ml	lime juice
10 ml	omega nutrition apple cider vinegar
1/4 tsp	clove powder
2 tsp	sea salt
50 ml	Omega Nutrition extra virgin olive oil
1/4 tsp	allspice
1 tsp	chili flakes

Serves 12

Nutrition Facts per Serving:
Calories 60, Carbohydrate
7g, Protein 0g, Fat 4g,
Fibre 1g, Sodium 330g

Method

1. In a heavy sauce pan on medium heat, stew onions in olive oil for approximately 15 minutes.

2. Add in all remaining ingredients except mint and return to heat, stirring constantly for 35 – 40 minutes.

3. Remove from heat, chill and serve with your favourite white meat or fish. Also makes a good glazing agent for roasts.

Escarole Salad
with Warm Dressing

Ingredients

4 tbsp	Omega Nutrition extra virgin olive oil
1/2	large white onion, chopped
5	small prunes, diced
2 tbsp	Omega Nutrition apple cider vinegar
2 tbsp	Omega Nutrition balsamic vinegar
1	head escarole endive, washed and cut
1	small gala apple, cubed
2 tsp	fresh thyme, chopped
100 g	sliced almonds

Serves 6

Nutrition Facts per Serving:
Calories 220, Carbohydrate 14g, Protein 5g, Fat 18g, Fibre 6g, Sodium 25mg

Method

1. In a frying pan, heat the oil and brown onion on medium high heat.

2. When starting to brown, add prunes and almonds and continue sautéing for approximately 7 – 10 minutes. Add vinegars, thyme and apples.

3. Add dressing to escarole. Toss well and salt to taste.

Focus on Nutrition:
Long overlooked, prunes are high in fibre, iron and antioxidants – as antioxidant rich as blueberries!

Hearty Millet Soup

Ingredients

1	small butternut squash
1	large onion, diced
2	carrots, diced
1	small fennel (or half large), diced
1	can lentils (540 ml)
1	can chick peas (398 ml)
1 tbsp	Omega Nutrition extra virgin olive oil
1 cup	millet
5 cups	water or stock (chicken or veggie)
1 cup	white wine
4	medium tomatoes, diced
1/2 tsp	sea salt
	Omega Nutrition pumpkin seed oil to garnish

Serves 8

Nutrition Facts per Serving:
Calories 370, carbohydrate 64g, protein 13g, Fat 6g, Fibre 13g, Sodium 170mg

Method

1. Preheat oven to 400° F.

2. Cut the squash and roast for 30 minutes, then cube.

3. In a large saucepan, warm oil and brown onion, carrot, and fennel. When lightly browned, add white wine and millet, drained lentils, chick peas, and water (or stock).

4. Bring to a boil then reduce to simmer for approximately 45 minutes or until millet is cooked. Add salt.

5. Add fresh diced tomato and pumpkin seed oil to taste prior to serving.

Artichoke and Quinoa Stir Fry

Ingredients

1 1/2 cups	quinoa, rinsed
3 +1 cups	water
4	fresh large artichokes
3	celery stalks, diced small
2	small onions, sliced
6 tbsp	Omega Nutrition extra virgin olive oil
5 tbsp	lemon juice
3	green onions, chopped
3 +3 tbsp	chopped parsley

Serves 4

Nutrition Facts per Serving:
Calories 520, Carbohydrate 67g, Protein 15g, Fat 24g, Fibre 14g, Sodium 200mg

Method

1. Bring 3 cups water to a boil and add quinoa. Reduce to simmer for 10 – 12 minutes or until all water has been absorbed. Set aside.

2. Prepare artichokes by removing all outside leaves, tops and stems. Cut in half lengthwise, and remove beard-like fuzz from centre of artichoke. Place in water and add a drop of lemon juice to prevent leaves from turning dark.

3. In a large frying pan, heat olive oil on medium heat and brown celery and onion.

4. Remove artichokes from water and slice lengthwise. Add to frying pan and cook for approximately 5 minutes. Add 3 tbsp parsley; cook 3 – 4 more minutes. Then add 1 cup water.

5. Increase heat to medium-high. When liquid has reduced by half, add lemon juice and cook for 2 – 3 more minutes. Add quinoa, remaining parsley, green onions and sauté for another minute.

Focus on Nutrition:
Quinoa, the high protein
"super grain", is actually a member
of the spinach family.

Buckwheat Crepes

Rice Mixture Ingredients

1/2 cup	brown rice
1 1/2 cups	water
1	bunch chard, chopped
1	medium russet potato, cubed
1 pinch	salt
250 g	grated cave-aged Gruyere

Crepes Ingredients

2	medium eggs
1 cup	Anita's Organic buckwheat flour
1 3/4 cup	Dairyland Organic 2% milk
1 pinch	salt
1 tbsp	Omega Nutrition extra virgin olive oil

Serves 6

Nutrition Facts per Serving:
Calories 430, Carbohydrate 43g, Protein 23g, Fat 20g, Fibre 5g, Sodium 340mg

Preheat oven to 400° F.

Method for rice mixture

1. Bring water to a boil; add pinch of salt, rice and return to boil. Simmer covered for 25 minutes. Add chard and potato. Stir and cover until all liquid is absorbed. Remove from heat and chill. Once chilled, mix in 3/4 of the cheese.

Method for crepes

1. In a large bowl combine flour, eggs, milk and pinch of salt. Leave sitting at room temperature for at least 10 – 15 minutes.

2. Dip the corner of a piece of paper towel into the olive oil and lightly coat the entire bottom of a small non-stick 6 inch frying pan. Heat on medium/med-high and pour approx 1/4 cup of mixture (depending on size of fry-pan) and move pan around to spread evenly on whole surface.

3. Within 40 – 50 seconds the crepe will be ready to flip; leave 5 – 10 seconds on 2nd side, and remove from pan. Mixture should make about 10 – 12 crepes.

Method to assemble

Scoop 2 – 3 tbsp of rice cheese mixture into center of crepe and roll. Place in lightly greased Pyrex. When all crepes are rolled in Pyrex, sprinkle with remaining cheese and bake for 25 minutes. Delicious served with radicchio or Belgian endive salad.

Focus on Nutrition:
Buckwheat is not wheat; it is
actually the fruit of a plant
related to rhubarb.

Tuscan Squash Risotto

Ingredients

1 1/2 L	vegetable or chicken stock
1 1/2 cups	cooked squash, such as buttercup
4 tbsp	Omega Nutrition Extra virgin olive oil
1/2	onion, chopped
1 cup	celery, diced small
2 cups	Arborio or Carnaroli rice
150 ml	white wine
1 tbsp	fresh rosemary, chopped
150 g	freshly grated Parmigiano Reggiano
100 g	Brie
1/2 tsp	salt
	cracked pepper

Serves 4

Nutrition Facts per Serving:
Calories 510, Carbohydrate 15g, Protein 33g, Fat 31g, Fibre 1g, Sodium 2380mg

Method

1. In a medium pot, bring vegetable stock to boil and keep hot.

2. In a heavy bottomed pot, heat oil on medium heat and brown onion and celery.

3. Add rice, stirring vigorously for about 3 1/2 minutes or rice is extremely hot.

4. Add previously roasted squash pulp and continue to stir vigorously.

5. Add wine, a little at a time, and stir. When wine has evaporated, start adding hot stock slowly, not more than 2 ladles at a time, while continuing to stir.

6. 15 minutes into cooking, add rosemary.

7. When rice has reached desired tenderness (Italian Risotto would be al dente, some prefer it softer) add cheeses, cracked pepper and stir.

8. Let rest for a few moments and then serve.

9. If desired, garnish each plate with a little extra shredded cheese and a few drops of pumpkin seed oil.

Leftovers can be turned into small patties and pan-fried the following day for beautiful risotto cakes!

 *Focus on Nutrition:*
Slash the sodium in this recipe by
substituting a low sodium broth.

Squash and Orange Soup

Ingredients

3	large carrots, peeled and cut in 1 – 2 inch pieces
1	large onion, cut in eighths
1 tbsp +2 tbsp	Omega Nutrition extra virgin olive oil
6 tsp	Luc Bergeron organic maple syrup
1	ripe squash, (acorn, butternut, banana, etc) quartered (2lbs)
1/4 tsp	ground cinnamon
1/4 tsp	salt
1 litre	water
1 cup	orange juice

Serves 6

Nutrition Facts per Serving:
Calories 300, Carbohydrates 52g, Protein 4g, Fat 11g, Fibre 5g, Sodium 210mg

Method

1. Preheat oven to 375° F.

2. In a medium bowl, toss carrots and onions with 1 tbsp olive oil and 1 tsp of maple syrup. Transfer to a baking sheet.

3. Remove seeds from squash and brush pieces with 2 tsp of maple syrup. Place on the baking sheet with carrots and onions and bake for 50 minutes.

4. Remove from oven, transferring carrots and onions into heavy bottomed soup pot with 2 tbsp of olive oil. Cook on medium high for 10 minutes.

5. Add cinnamon and salt, stirring until onions and carrots are coated.

6. With a spoon, remove squash pulp from skin and add to soup pot. Stir and cook for 5 minutes with onions and carrots.

7. Add water and bring to a boil. Reduce heat and let simmer for 25 minutes.

8. Stir in orange juice and remaining maple syrup. Puree soup ingredients with a hand held immersion blender.

9. Check seasoning and add more cinnamon and salt if desired.

 *Focus on Nutrition:*
The carrots and squash in this soup
deliver a potent dose of beta
carotene, a vitamin A precursor,
to promote healthy skin.

Pasta with Hemp and Cheddar Pesto

Ingredients

1/3 cup	fresh mint (28 g)
3	garlic cloves
5 tbsp	Mum's Original hemp seed oil
2 cups	Mum's Original hulled hemp seeds
1 tsp	black pepper
1/2 tsp (+1 – 2 tbsp for pasta water)	salt
1 tbsp	Omega Nutrition balsamic vinegar
150 g	extra aged cheddar, shredded
4 tbsp	Omega Nutrition extra virgin olive oil
3	small zucchini or 2 large, cubed
500 g	Prairie Harvest or San Zenone short pasta (penne, farfalle, etc)

Serves 6

Nutrition Facts per Serving:
Calories 660, Carbohydrate 73g, Protein 25g, Fat 44g, Fibre 13g, Sodium 360mg

Method

1. To make the pesto: In food processor, blend mint, garlic cloves, hemp oil, hemp seeds, pepper, 1/2 tsp salt and balsamic vinegar until smooth.

2. In large bowl, combine the pesto with shredded cheddar.

3. In a large frying pan over medium heat, heat olive oil and sauté zucchini until golden brown.

4. Fill large pot with water and bring to a boil. Add remaining salt and pasta, cooking until slightly firm or al dente.

5. Scoop 2 or 3 tbsp of the pasta water into pesto mixture and mix thoroughly, creating smooth pesto.

6. Strain pasta and combine with sauce and zucchini. Enjoy while hot.

 *Nutrition Tip: Hemp seeds are rich in protein and omega 3 fatty acids to help soothe inflammation.*

Warkentin Organic Farm
Matsqui BC

Ron and Bette Warkentin purchased a 10 acre lot on Matsqui prairie in November of 1988 as the home of their blueberry farm. They had their work cut out for them: other than a house and couple of outbuildings, the entire property was in pasture. Their first planting of blueberries in May 1989 was only about 3 acres. Quickly growing apprehensive about the chemicals typically used by conventional growers, Ron and Bette made the decision to transition to organic in 1990. The Warkentins had always grown their home gardens organically and they wanted the food they produced for other families to be healthy and chemical free – something to be proud of. They joined the Association for Regenerative Agriculture while the organization was still in its infancy as it spoke to the Warkentins' vision of sustainable agricultural practices. The entire farm achieved certified organic status in 1993.

In 1996, the Warkentin Organic Farm started supplying the West 16th Choices store with fresh blueberries. Soon after, Steve Lockhart asked Ron and Bette to supply the entire Choices chain with fresh and frozen blueberries year round, which the Warkentin Organic Farm has been doing ever since. Ron has remarked on this long term partnership, "It has been a pleasure to build and grow together with a like-minded business. Our commitment is to work hard at continuing this relationship and sustain it as a successful team effort. We are growers and Choices is our major customer in the retail market." In addition to blueberries, the farm supplies Choices Market with a custom berry mixture consisting of frozen blueberries, blackberries, strawberries and raspberries that also includes fruit from other organic berry farms.

Committed to sharing their knowledge, Ron and Bette also mentor other growers who want to transition their farms into organic and have formed a partnership with some of these growers to help the Warkentin Organic Farm supply the local organic blueberry market. These include Ron and Bette's son Damon, long-time family friends Dale and Cathy Larson and Damon's good friend Brad Nedimovich. With the help of these partner farms, the Warkentin Organic Farm can offer more blueberry varieties over a longer season. The farm also grows a thornless blackberry variety and has grown strawberries in the past. The Warkentin Organic Farm is committed to producing high quality food products in the spirit of a family owned and operated business.

Chocolate Ricotta Tartlettes

Ingredients

15	2-inch unsweetened frozen tart shells
2	egg yolks
2 tbsp	honey
1/4 tsp	grated lemon rind
1/2 tsp	vanilla
1/3 cup	Cuisine Camino cocoa powder
1/2 cup	ricotta cheese
30	Cuisine Camino chocolate chips
	whipping cream or mascarpone for garnish, if desired

Serves 15 tartlettes

Nutrition Facts per Serving:
Calories 140, Carbohydrates 13g, Protein 3g, Fat 8g, Fibre 1g, Sodium 60mg

Method

1. Preheat oven to 350° F.

2. Pre-bake shells for 7 – 8 minutes. Set aside to cool.

3. Mix yolks, honey, lemon rind and vanilla in a bowl.

4. Slowly work cocoa into the mixture, then mix in ricotta.

5. Pour mixture into cooled shells and add 2 chocolate chips per tartlette.

6. Bake for 20 minutes. Chill and serve with a small dollop of whipping cream or mascarpone, if desired.

Choose Fair Trade Cocoa, Sugar, Tea and Coffee to help support a fair wage and livelihood for those who grow our favourite treats.

Onion and Tomato Beef Stew

Ingredients

2 tbsp	Omega Nutrition extra virgin olive oil
2 lbs	Diamond Willow organic beef stewing meat, cubed (900 g)
4	large onions, sliced
2	bay leaves
1 tbsp	ground cinnamon, heaping
1 cup	red wine
	salt and pepper to taste
1	can diced tomatoes (790 mL)

Serves 8

Nutrition Facts per Serving:
Calories 410, Carbohydrates 22g, Protein 33g, Fat 18g, Fibre 5g, Sodium 290mg

Method

1. Over medium-high heat, heat oil in large heavy bottomed soup pot and brown beef.

2. When beef is golden on all sides add onions and continue browning for approximately 25 minutes.

3. Add bay leaves, ground cinnamon and red wine. Simmer uncovered for 10 minutes. Season lightly with salt and pepper.

4. Add canned tomatoes and simmer on medium-low, covered, for at least 3 hours stirring regularly every 10 – 15 minutes. Depending on quality and variety of beef meat you may have to stew longer to obtain desired tenderness.

5. For variety, try adding other ingredients like sautéed mushrooms or fresh vegetables.

The stew is excellent reheated and served with your favorite starches (potatoes, rice, polenta, couscous, etc)

West Coast Yam Chowder

Ingredients

2 L	water
2	yams, cubed
2	sweet potatoes, cubed
2	russet potatoes, cubed
1/2	head roasted garlic
2	red onions, chopped finely
1	medium carrot, cubed
3	stalks celery, cubed
1	leek, sliced
3 tbsp	Omega Nutrition extra virgin olive oil
5 tbsp	Luc Bergeron organic maple syrup
2 tbsp	kelp, minced
	coarse pepper to taste
4 tbsp	Omega Nutrition High – O sunflower seed oil
	mizithra cheese or your favourite cheese

Serves 8

Nutrition Facts per Serving:
Calories 280, Carbohydrate 42g, Protein 3g, Fat 12g, Fibre 5g, Sodium 55mg

Method

1. Preheat oven to 425° F.

2. In a heavy bottomed soup pot, boil water and add 1/2 of the yams, 1/2 of the sweet potatoes, all of the russet potatoes and roasted garlic.

3. Let boil until reduced to almost half then liquefy with a hand blender.

4. In a separate bowl, mix together remaining yams, onion, carrot, celery, leek, olive oil and maple syrup. Place on a cookie sheet and roast for 25 minutes until golden brown.

5. Add roasted vegetables to the liquid soup then stir in kelp and pepper.

6. Before serving stir in sunflower seed oil and a handful of grated mizithra cheese if desired.

 *Nutrition Tip: A Canadian favourite, flavourful maple syrup also contains trace amounts of calcium, iron and potassium.*

No Egg "Egg Salad"

Ingredients

1 tsp	turmeric
3/4	package Soyganic extra firm tofu, crumbled
2/3 cup	mayo, regular or vegan
1/2 tbsp	dijon mustard
1 tsp	lemon juice
2	green onions, chopped
8	baby pickles, chopped
1	package Mandarin Soyfoods pressed tofu, chopped
	salt to taste

Fills 5 sandwiches

Nutrition Facts per Serving:
Calories (filling only) 230,
Carbohydrates 10g,
Protein 22g, Fat 12g,
Fibre 2g, Sodium 1400mg

Method

1. Sprinkle turmeric on crumbled tofu and set aside.

2. In a large bowl combine mayo, mustard, lemon juice, green onions, and pickles.

3. Mix in both tofus and chill for at least 30 minutes.

4. Serve on bread or wraps of your choice.

*Nutrition Tip:
Slash the sodium in this recipe by
omitting the pickles.*

Winter

In our fair province, winter is more likely to mean cold, rainy days as opposed to sugar-coated landscapes and blue sky.

Such dark days require nourishing, fortifying fare. Sip a steaming mug of cocoa and watch the rain dance outside the window. Find solace in warming stews brimming with local squash, kale and parsnip, scented with sage and rosemary. Bundle up; find a puddle and splash away knowing that a simmering pot of soup is waiting for you at home. Feast with friends and family to celebrate the holidays that brighten this time of year like no other. Now is the time when the locavore's hard work pays off. Cellars are full of root veggies to bake and stew and delectable jams, chutneys and preserves to slather over thick slices of bread on a Sunday morning. These foods bring comfort and a reminder that spring is just around the corner.

Savoury Winter Strudel

Ingredients

1	russet potato, peeled and cubed
1/2	medium carrot, peeled and diced
1	apple, thinly sliced and cut into 1 1/2 inch square pieces
100 g	Port Salut or favorite cheese, thinly sliced
7	sheets whole wheat phyllo pastry
1/3 cup	Omega Nutrition virgin coconut oil
1 pinch	sea salt

Makes 21 strudel

Nutrition Facts per Serving:
Calories 60, Carbohydrate
3g, Protein 1g, Fat 5g, Fibre
1g, Sodium 75mg

Method

1. Preheat oven to 375° F.

2. Place potatoes and carrots in small saucepan, bring to a boil and cook until tender. Strain, and mash, and add seasoning to taste.

3. Melt coconut oil. On a clean and dry counter top, lay pastry sheet in a horizontal position in front of you. Cut 3 vertical strips, and place a teaspoon of mash at the center of the bottom of each strip. Top with a slice of apple and thin slice of cheese. Brush the rest of the strip with melted coconut oil. Fold left and right side of strip over the mixture and brush once again with coconut oil. Roll completely and brush once more.

4. Bake for 15 minutes. Serve warm or cold, with wine jelly.

Focus on Nutrition: An apple a day just might keep the doctor away! Apples contain soluble fibre for your heart and glutathione, the "super" antioxidant.

Winter Vegetable Stew

Ingredients

4 tbsp	Omega Nutrition extra virgin olive oil
1	bunch black kale, chopped
2	large Ccarrots, diced small
1	small turnip, diced small
4	small parsnips, diced small
1	small leek, sliced
1	large garlic clove, chopped
28 g	fresh thyme (1 package), chopped
1 1/3 cups	organic orange lentils, presoaked
1	small can kidney beans, rinsed and drained
1	small can navy beans, rinsed and drained
1	small can garbanzo beans, rinsed and drained
2 L	water or stock
1/2 tsp	sea salt
200 g	freshly grated Romano cheese (optional)
	pepper to taste

Serves 8

Nutrition Facts per Serving:
Calories 530, Carbohydrate 56g, Protein 29g, Fat 15g, Fibre 16g, Sodium 720mg

Method

1. In a heavy bottomed soup pot, heat olive oil and stew black kale for 15 minutes on low heat.

2. Add carrot, turnip, parsnips, leek, garlic, and half the thyme. Continue stewing for another 15 minutes.

3. Add all the beans and the pre-soaked lentils with stock or water.

4. Bring to a boil; simmer until all ingredients are tender, stirring regularly.

5. Add salt and remaining thyme right before serving. Add cheese to individual bowls before you serve. Do not add cheese to the pot if you are freezing or saving leftover soup in the fridge.

Sunchoke Soup

Ingredients

4 tbsp +2 tbsp	Omega Nutrition extra virgin olive oil
1/2 lb	shallots, chopped
1	large garlic clove, chopped
2 lbs	sunchokes, washed and coarsely sliced
1 cup	white wine
2 L	vegetable or chicken stock or water
	small bunch flat leaf parsley, chopped
1/2 tbsp	sea salt
1/2 cup	Olympic Organic plain 2% yogurt

Serves 8

Nutrition Facts per Serving:
Calories 140, Carbohydrate 6g, Protein 1g, Fat 10g, Fibre 0g, Sodium 380mg

Method

1. In a heavy sauce-pan, heat 4 tbsp of olive oil and lightly brown chopped shallots.

2. Add garlic and sliced sunchokes. Stew for approximately 15 minutes on medium heat. When sunchokes start to brown, add wine.

3. When wine has reduced by half, add stock and bring to a boil. Reduce heat and simmer for approximately 25 minutes, stirring consistently.

4. When sunchokes have reached the consistency of a boiled potato, puree soup with a hand held blender. When smooth, add salt and parsley.

5. Prior to serving, add a dollop of yogurt and drizzle with remaining olive oil. Add pepper to taste.

 *Focus on Nutrition: Freshly chopped garlic has potent phytochemicals that help your body eliminate potentially cancer causing toxins.*

Asian Turkey Chowder

Ingredients

2	carrots, 1 whole and 1 diced
2	stalks celery, 1 whole and 1 diced
1	onion, 1/2 whole and 1/2 diced
1	small leek, white diced and green whole
1/4 cup	frozen peas
1/4 cup	frozen corn
1/2 cup	potatoes, diced
1	can coconut milk (400 ml)
1/2 cup	dry white wine
1/2	lime, juiced
3 tbsp	Omega Nutrition virgin coconut oil
3 tbsp	cilantro, chopped and stems reserved
2 cups	turkey meat, diced
3	peppercorns
	salt and pepper to taste

Serves 6

> **Nutrition Facts per Serving:**
> Calories 370, Carbohydrate
> 14g, Protein 18g, Fat 26g,
> Fibre 2g, Sodium 105mg

Turkey Stock Method

1. To make your own turkey stock, cover turkey bones with cold water and add the whole carrot, celery, leek green, cilantro stems and peppercorns. Bring to a rapid boil and simmer for 3 – 4 hours.

2. Strain and skim fat off stock then simmer to reduce to 3 L. You can also substitute 3 L of store bought chicken stock and proceed with remainder of recipe.

Chowder Method

1. In a soup pot, heat coconut oil on medium heat and brown onions, celery, carrot and leek. Add lime juice and white wine and let evaporate.

2. Add stock and bring to a boil; once boiling, add potatoes.

3. When potatoes are cooked, add turkey, corn and peas and return to boil.

4. Add coconut milk, cilantro and check the seasoning.

Smoked Cheddar Dip

Ingredients

150 g	smoked cheddar, grated
1	head garlic
2	green onions, finely chopped
1 tbsp	fresh lemon juice
1 cup	Olympic sour cream
10	drops Tabasco
1/2 cup	mayo

Serves 8 as a snack or appetizer

Nutrition Facts per Serving:
Calories 160, Carbohydrate 5g, Protein 6g, Fat 10g, Fibre 0g, Sodium 55mg

Method

1. Roast garlic at 400° F for 35 – 40 minutes or until soft to touch. Squeeze roasted garlic into a bowl and allow to cool.

2. Mash garlic with a spoon then add all remaining ingredients, mix and chill until ready to serve. Serve with crackers, pita, chips or bread.

 *Focus on Nutrition: lighten this delicious dip by using light (not fat free) mayo and sour cream for fewer calories and less saturated fat.*

Potato Gnocchi

Ingredients

2 3/4 lb	Russet potatoes (about 4 large)
1/4 cup	freshly grated Parmesan Cheese
2	large eggs
1 pinch	sea salt
1 pinch	nutmeg
2 1/4 cup	Anita's Organic unbleached white flour

Serves 6 servings

Nutrition Facts per Serving:
Calories 420, Carbohydrate 77g, Protein 16g, Fat 5g, Fibre 6g, Sodium 400mg

Method

1. In a large amount of cold water, boil potatoes with skin on until soft. Peel potatoes while still warm. Mash with a potato ricer or hand held potato masher.

2. Put mashed potatoes in very large bowl and add the parmesan, eggs, salt and nutmeg.

3. Add flour slowly and mix gently until uniform, making sure not to over work. Let rest for 15 – 20 minutes.

4. Flour a working surface so gnocchi do not stick to counter. Cut slices of dough and form into finger size "sausages". Cut sausages into thumb nail size pieces and try to form shell like shapes by pressing onto the fork. Let gnocchi air dry on working surface for 1 hour.

5. Cook in boiling salted water in small batches. When gnocchi rise to the surface of the water, they are ready.

6. Scoop gnocchi with strainer spoon — do not strain in a pasta strainer.

7. Serve with your favourite sauce.

After air drying, gnocchi can be frozen for later use and should be cooked from the frozen state – do not thaw.

Thai-style Root Vegetable Stir Fry

Ingredients

2	turnips, cut into 1 1/2 cm sticks
1	bunch beets, cut into 1 1/2 cm sticks
1	carrot, sliced
4	sun-chokes, roughly cubed
1	medium onion, sliced
1	bunch cilantro, roughly chopped
2	limes, juiced
3 tbsp	Omega Nutrition virgin coconut oil
1	jalapeno (optional)

Serves 2

Nutrition Facts per Serving:
Calories 370, Carbohydrate 45g, Protein 6g, Fat 21g, Fibre 12g, Sodium 280mg

Method

1. Heat coconut oil in wok or large non-stick frying pan on high heat.

2. Gradually add turnip, beets, carrots, sun-chokes and onions, maintaining heat level between each addition. Stir frequently.

3. When vegetables start to brown, season and add jalapeno, if desired. Slowly add lime juice, maintaining heat.

4. Toss with cilantro. Serve stir fry on its own or with a steamed whole grain.

Focus on Nutrition: Sunchokes, or Jerusalem Artichokes, are rich in inulin – a prebiotic fibre.

Polenta Medallions with Caramelized Duck

Ingredients

1	duck breast, approx 220 – 250 g
1 1/2 tbsp	coarse sea salt
1 1/2 tbsp	brown sugar
1	roll pre-cooked polenta
1	shallot
1/4 cup	dried cranberries, packed measure
1 1/2	large oranges, 1 juiced, other half thinly sliced
1/4 tsp	ground cloves
1/2 tbsp	Omega Nutrition extra virgin olive oil

Makes 30 bite sized medallions

Nutrition Facts per Serving:
Calories 25, Carbohydrate 4g, Protein 1g, Fat 0g, Fibre 0g, Sodium 70mg

Method

1. Preheat oven to 400° F.

2. Score duck skin 3 or 4 times in each direction. Place duck breast on a plate. Mix sugar and salt and cover skin with salt/sugar mixture. Refrigerate for 1 hour 45 minutes, then wash and pat dry.

3. Heat a heavy skillet on med-high and when hot place duck breast skin down, allowing to cook 3 or 4 minutes or until caramelized. Flip over and cook other side for 2 – 3 minutes. Bake for 10 minutes then allow to rest for at least 15 – 20 minutes before cutting.

4. In the skillet, brown polenta medallions (approx 15 slices per roll) in the duck drippings and then cut the medallions in half to produce 30 half moon slices.

5. In a separate small sauce-pan, heat olive oil and lightly brown shallots, add cranberries and cloves and cook for a few minutes. Add orange juice and allow reduction until nearly dry.

6. Thinly slice duck on a 45 degree angle. Place half a slice of duck on polenta medallion. Add a triangular slice of skinless orange and top with a small tsp of cranberry compote. Serve at room temperature.

Gnocchi Quattro Formaggi

Ingredients

100 g	Grana Padano or Parmigiano Reggiano, grated
100 g	Fontina cheese, grated
100 g	Emmenthal cheese, grated
100 g	White Stilton, cubed (or Gorgonzola)
1 cup	Dairyland whipping cream
1 kg/2 lbs	gnocchi
1 tbsp	sea salt for cooking water

Serves 6

> **Nutrition Facts per Serving:**
> Calories 620, Carbohydrate 49g, protein 28g, Fat 34g, Fibre 4g, Sodium 1500mg

Method

1. In a heavy saucepan, heat cream on medium-high heat and gently combine all cheeses until completely melted.

2. Bring abundant water to a boil with sea salt. Add gnocchi and stir. Gnocchi will be ready in approximately 3 minutes. Remove with a meshed spoon and toss with cheese sauce.

Mediterranean Style
Stuffed Potatoes

Ingredients

3	large russet potatoes, baked and chilled
150 g	smoked cod (Alaskan black sable fish)
2 tbsp	fresh sage, chopped
150 g	Happy Days goat feta
3	sun dried tomatoes, diced
1 tbsp	lemon juice
2 tbsp	Omega Nutrition extra virgin olive oil

Serves 6

Nutrition Facts per Serving:
Calories 280, Carbohydrate
37g, Protein 12g, Fat 11g,
Fibre 6g, Sodium 280mg

Method

1. Preheat oven to 375° F.

2. Cut potatoes in half, lengthwise. Spoon out the pulp and place in a separate bowl.

3. Mix feta and sun dried tomatoes in a small bowl.

4. Mix cubed cod, sage, most of the feta (keep 4 tbsp), lemon juice and olive oil. Work mass in steel bowl until well blended.

5. Fill potato shells and top with remaining feta. Bake for 25 – 30 minutes.

Dairy Free
Baked Macaroni Alfredo

Ingredients

2 cups	Natura unsweetened rice milk
1 tbsp +2 tbsp	Omega Nutrition extra virgin olive oil
4	cloves roasted garlic, chopped
4 tbsp	rice flour
4 tbsp	parsley, chopped
1/2 tsp	sea salt
1 cup	vegan mozzarella, shredded
1 tsp	black pepper
1 cup	Prairie Harvest Organic macaroni or San Zenone Brown Rice Pasta
1 pinch	nutmeg
2	Roma tomatoes, finely diced

Serves 4

Nutrition Facts per Serving:
Calories 460, Carbohydrate 40g, Protein 11g, Fat 29g, Fibre 3g, Sodium 880mg

Method

1. Preheat oven to 375º F.

2. In a heavy saucepan, heat 1 tbsp of oil. Add roasted garlic and when it starts sizzling, add 2 tbsp chopped parsley and cook for 5 minutes.

3. Add rice milk, salt, and rice flour while whisking. Bring to a boil and then simmer on medium heat for 4 – 5 minutes, while stirring constantly.

4. Add vegan cheese and a pinch of nutmeg and pepper. With immersion (hand held) blender, liquefy into a smooth sauce. Add remaining parsley and olive oil.

5. In a separate pot, cook the noodles in abundant salted water. Strain well and mix with sauce in a Pyrex oven dish, top with diced tomato and bake for 20 minutes.

Polenta with Wild Mushrooms

Ingredients

3 cups	oyster mushrooms, sliced
2 cups	leeks, chopped
3 tbsp	Omega Nutrition extra virgin olive oil
1	large garlic clove, sliced
1	bunch flat leaf parsley, chopped
1	lemon, juiced
1/2 +1/2 tsp	salt
6 cups	water
2 cups	corn meal (corn grits or polenta)
pinch	cinnamon
1/2 tsp	sea salt
180 g	freshly grated Parmigiano Reggiano or Grana Padano

Serves 6

Nutrition Facts per Serving:
Calories 390, Carbohydrate 50g, Protein 17g, Fat 15g, Fibre 7g, Sodium 1g

Method

1. In a large frying pan, warm oil and brown leeks and garlic, stirring, for 15 minutes. Add oyster mushrooms and sauté for 15 more minutes. Next add salt, parsley and lemon juice and remove from heat.

2. Bring water to a boil and add salt. Whisk vigorously while pouring polenta, a little at a time, into water. Reduce heat, making sure the mixture is still slowly bubbling and stir constantly with a very long, sturdy wooden spoon for 30 minutes. Lastly, mix in cinnamon, grated cheese, and mushrooms.

Focus on nutrition: cinnamon is considered a warming spice in the Ayurvedic tradition and may help to stabilize blood sugars.

Kasha and Salmon Cakes

Ingredients

1 cup	kasha (toasted buckwheat groats)
1	green onion, finely diced
2	small green zucchini, small cubed
1 tbsp +1 tbsp	Omega Nutrition extra virgin olive oil
1 tsp	lemon rind, chopped
2 tbsp	lemon juice
2/3	can Raincoast wild pink salmon
2	eggs
1 tsp +1 tsp	sea salt
	fresh cracked black pepper to taste

Serves 12 cakes

> **Nutrition Facts per Serving:**
> Calories 80, Carbohydrates 4g, Protein 7g, Fat 4.5, Fibre 1g, Sodium 480mg

Method

1. Preheat oven to 375° F.

2. Bring 3 L of water to a boil, add salt and kasha. Cook for approximately 10 – 12 minutes until kasha is tender. Strain and cool.

3. In a small frying pan on medium-high heat, sauté' zucchini in 1 tbsp olive oil until starting to brown.

4. In a medium sized bowl, mash the canned salmon including bone and skin with a fork. Add green onion, lemon juice and lemon rind, 1 tbsp olive oil, black pepper and zucchini. Mix. Add 2 eggs and mix well.

5. Add cold cooked kasha, mix and form 12 small patties (about 2 1/2 or 3 inch diameter) with an ice cream scoop or by hand. Bake for 18 – 20 minutes.

Myers Organic Farms
"Fresh, Local,
And Certified Organic"

Nearly 15 years ago, Bob and Marlene Myers purchased two acres of farmland nestled in Aldergrove, BC. Originally, the land was seen as a trial project, an opportunity to experiment with growing and harvesting small crops of organic produce. Over time, their nugget of land has grown into over 60 acres, and Myers Organic Farms is now a supplier of some of the finest quality organic produce grown in the Fraser Valley.

Every year, the Myerses consistently harvest a beautiful array of organically grown produce: lettuces, kales, chards, radishes, beets, their own spinach blend, herbs, garlic, shallots, strawberries, raspberries, rhubarb, currants, corn and even edible flowers.

Still entirely a family-run business, Bob, Marlene and their son Brock are the back-bone of the operation. Each plays an integral role ensuring the success of the farm, and with the commitment and dedication of their 23 employees, Myers Organic Farms continues to thrive.

Bob manages the daily operations of the farm and designates the tasks that need to take place throughout the day. When he's not personally hauling in every box of harvested produce, you can find Bob tilling a patch of land for another planting, preparing trays for seedlings in the greenhouse or laying mulch for the next new transplants.

The logistics of the business are left to Marlene, who handles the inner operations of the farm. She is responsible for running the office, managing the cooler and warehouse and marketing the produce.

Brock has the distinct honour of being the on-site master mechanic. Rarely a day goes by where Brock isn't welding or repairing a piece of machinery. He also earns his keep by tending to and preparing the soil, seeding and cultivating by machine, weeding, trimming the buffer zones, grading the roads and maintaining the irrigation systems.

As Myers Organic Farms has taken root and flourished, so has the passion for what they do for the community. Marlene Myers explains: "It feels great to know that you are putting delicious, healthy, organic food on a lot of tables in your community. We're part of a sustainable system that will preserve the land for our children's children. It is a huge undertaking that we are very proud to be a part of."

Winter Greens Risotto

Ingredients

1/2	onion, chopped
1 tbsp +2 tbsp	Omega Nutrition extra virgin olive oil
1	can black soya beans
1	bunch collard greens, leaves sliced and stems chopped
1	bunch lacinato kale, roughly chopped
1	pinch chili flakes
1	pinch salt
1	cup quinoa
500 ml	chicken or veggie stock
1/4 cup	Italian parsley, chopped
100 g	aave aged Emmental, shredded

Serves 4

Nutrition Facts per Serving:
Calories 570, Carbohydrate
53g, Protein 31g, Fat 28g,
Fibre 11g, Sodium 400mg

Method

1. Place 1 tbsp olive oil in a heavy sauce-pan on medium heat and brown onions.

2. Add chili flakes, kale, and the chopped collard stems. Stew for 15 minutes, while constantly stirring.

3. Add quinoa and stew for 5 more minutes while stirring. Add collard leaves and continue stewing for 5 – 8 minutes more.

4. Add salt, black soya beans and stock and continue stewing, stirring constantly for approximately 20 minutes. When all of the liquid is absorbed and quinoa feels tender but not mushy, turn heat off and add remaining olive oil and shredded cheese and stir well. Allow to rest 5 – 10 minutes before serving.

Focus on Nutrition: Quinoa is considered a complete protein, meaning it has adequate amounts of all essential amino acids, including lysine.

Hearty Veggie Shepherd's Pie

Ingredients

2 lbs	yams (about 2 large), peeled and large cubed
2	medium carrots, diced
1/2	large onion, diced
2	stalks celery, diced
2 tbsp +1 tbsp	Omega Nutrition extra virgin olive oil
10	shiitake mushrooms, cubed
2 tbsp	gen mai miso
1 cup	water
1/4 cup	red wine (or water)
2	cans your favourite beans, drained and rinsed (540 ml each)
1 tbsp	paprika
1 cup	frozen peas

Serves 6

Nutrition Facts per Serving:
Calories 410, Carbohydrate 77g, Protein 10g, Fat 8g, Fibre 14g,, Sodium 680mg

Method

1. Preheat oven to 400° F.

2. Boil yams in abundant water and mash. Salt to taste.

3. On medium high, sauté carrot, onion and celery for 10 minutes in 2 tbsp oil. Add shiitakes and miso. Cook for another 10 minutes adding wine, a little at a time.

4. Add paprika and beans. Cook and add remaining water while mashing beans for approximately 15 minutes. Season to taste.

5. Pour mixture in 8 x 8 Pyrex. Sprinkle frozen peas over mixture and top with mashed yams. "Paint" yams with a 1 tbsp of olive oil.

6. Bake for 30 minutes.

 *Focus on Nutrition:*
Miso is a fermented soy paste
that offers a vegan source of
vitamin B12...but beware of the
high sodium content!

Cream of Mushroom Soup

Ingredients

1lb	button mushrooms
1lb	Portobello or Shiitake mushrooms
1	medium onion, chopped
1	stalk celery, chopped
1	large garlic clove, chopped
20 g	dried mushrooms (Porcini or wild mix, steeped in boiling water)
1	pinch cinnamon
1 1/2 tsp	sea salt
1/2 cup	red wine
3 tbsp	Omega Nutrition olive oil
1 tbsp	parsley, chopped
5 cups	water
1/2 cup	rice
1 cup	Dairyland whipping cream

Serves 6

Nutrition Facts per Serving:
Calories 290, Carbohydrate 21g, Protein 5g, Fat 20g, Fibre 2g, Sodium 520mg

Method

1. In a heavy sauce-pan, sweat chopped onion, garlic and celery in olive oil until soft.

2. Add chopped mushrooms, cover and stew, stirring occasionally for 10 – 15 minutes. Add red wine, salt and cinnamon and stew for 5 more minutes.

4. Add water, bring to a boil then reduce to simmer for 10 more minutes. Add rice and boil for approximately 15 minutes or until rice is soft.

5. Puree with immersion (hand held) blender. Add chopped parsley, whipping cream, and cracked pepper to taste. Bring to a boil, stirring and then serve.

Blue Russian Potato and Corn Soup

Ingredients

1	large yellow onion, diced
1 lb	Blue Russian potatoes, cubed
2 cups	your favourite stock (chicken, beef or veggie)
1/4 cup	white wine
1 cup	water
1	corn cob (or 1/3 cup frozen or canned corn kernels)
1/2 tsp	sea salt
1 tbsp	Omega Nutrition extra virgin olive oil

Serves 4

Nutrition Facts per Serving:
Calories 140, Carbohydrate 27g, Protein 5g, Fat 4g, Fibre 3g, Sodium 640mg

Method

1. In a heavy saucepan, heat olive oil and brown onions. Next, add potatoes, wine, stock and water.

2. Bring to a boil, then reduce to simmer for approximately 20 minutes.

3. Remove kernels from raw cob and add to soup. Simmer for 5 more minutes.

4. Add salt and if desired freshly cracked pepper. Serve warm.

Gluten Free Chocolate Pudding

Ingredients

1/2 cup +2 cups	Natura rice milk
1/4 cup	corn starch
1/2 cup	Camino Cuisine cocoa powder
1/2 cup	brown sugar
5	egg yolks
1 tsp	vanilla extract
1	piece organic lemon zest

Serves 6

Nutrition Facts per Serving:
Calories 190, Carbohydrates 27g, Protein 4g, Fat 6g, Fibre 3g, Sodium 15mg

Method

1. In small bowl, mix 1/2 cup of rice milk with corn starch with a whisk, ensuring no lumps. Set aside.

2. In large heavy bottomed sauce-pan, mix cocoa, sugar, yolks and vanilla. Add 2 cups of rice milk and stir until all ingredients have dissolved.

3. Place on stove on medium high. Add lemon zest and continue stirring making sure that nothing sticks to bottom.

4. Bring to a boil, continuing to stir vigorously.

5. Give another quick whisk to rice milk and corn starch mixture making sure it is smooth and well mixed. Pour into boiling chocolate pudding, returning it to a boil until pudding is thick. Remember to stir constantly.

6. Remove from heat and pull out lemon zest. Pour pudding into individual serving bowls or one large bowl. Chill.

7. Recipe can be made vegan friendly without eggs. The result will be similar but less creamy.

Winter Beef Soup

Ingredients

1 1/2 lbs	Diamond Willow beef short ribs, cut into 3/4 inch cubes (650 grams)
1 tbsp	Omega Nutrition extra virgin olive oil
2	whole garlic cloves
2	large carrots, sliced
1	large turnip, diced
	salt and pepper to taste
1 L	water
1 L	beef or chicken stock
1	sprig fresh rosemary

Serves 6

Nutrition Facts per Serving:
Calories (without grain) 250,
Carbohydrate 7g, Protein
25g, Fat 14g, Fibre 1g,
Sodium 450mg

Method

1. Over medium-high heat, heat oil in large heavy bottomed soup pot. Brown beef and let stew for 20 minutes.

2. Add garlic, carrots, turnip and rosemary and stew on medium heat for 20 more minutes.

3. Add salt and pepper and pour in stock and water and bring to a fast simmer, cooking for 2 hours.

4. After 2 hours, beef should be tender and falling apart. Taste for rich flavour and add more salt and pepper if necessary.

5. If desired, add 1/4 cup of your favorite dry grain (quinoa, barley, kamut, etc) and continue simmering until grain is cooked.

Unbaked Beans

Ingredients

500 g	nitrate-free bacon, chopped
2	large onions, finely diced
1/4 tsp	cinnamon
3 tbsp	organic molasses
1/2	small can tomato paste (156 mls/5 oz)
3	cans your favourite beans (small red kidney, pinto, navy, etc), rinsed
1/4 tsp	salt
1/2 cup +3 cups	water

Serves 12

Nutrition Facts per Serving:
Calories 360, Carbohydrates 28g, Protein 13g, Fat 22g, Fibre 6g, Sodium 650mg

Method

1. In a heavy bottomed soup pot on medium heat, cook bacon for approximately 20 minutes. Drain fat and return to the stove.

2. Add onions and cinnamon. Stew for 20 minutes while stirring frequently.

3. Mix in molasses, tomato paste and 1/2 cup of water. Cook for 5 more minutes stirring often.

4. Add rinsed beans and remaining water and salt. Simmer, partially covered, for 1 hr making sure beans don't dry out too much.

5. If you prefer a sweeter version add 1/4 cup of Luc Bergeron organic maple syrup when adding the remaining water.

Nutrition Tip: Beans are an excellent source of soluble fibre to help lower blood cholesterol levels.

Tofu Parmigiana

Ingredients

5 tbsp	Omega Nutrition extra virgin olive oil
1 large	eggplant or 2 small, sliced lengthwise, 1/4 inch thick
1	package Soyganic firm or extra firm tofu, drained and sliced approx 1/4 inch thick
2	ripe medium tomatoes, finely diced
1	clove garlic, chopped
1 1/2 tsp	dried oregano
200 g	mozzarella, sliced
	salt
1/4 cup	freshly grated parmesan cheese (optional)

Serves 6

Nutrition Facts per Serving:
Calories 340, Carbohydrates 14g, Protein 21g, Fat 23g, Fibre 6g, Sodium 400mg

---

Method

1. Preheat oven to 375° F.

2. Heat olive oil in a large non-stick frying pan on medium-high heat. Pan fry eggplant until golden brown on each side. Remove eggplant and lay on paper towel to drain.

3. Return the pan back to burner, brown tofu on both sides. Remove from pan.

4. In a small bowl, combine tomato, garlic, oregano and a pinch of salt.

5. On a cookie sheet, layer one slice of tofu, small amount of tomato mixture, one slice of eggplant, another small amount of tomato mixture and finally one slice of mozzarella on top.

6. Fold the eggplant overtop of the tomato and mozzarella then top with a heaping teaspoon of tomato mixture.

7. Bake for 10 – 12 minutes. If desired, sprinkle parmesan cheese prior to baking.

8. Serve hot or at room temperature.

Roasted Pumpkin and Whole Wheat Lasagna

Ingredients

4 tbsp +1 tbsp	Omega Nutrition extra virgin olive oil
1 1/2 cups	shallots, chopped
3 cups	roasted pumpkin pulp
1 cup	white wine
1 1/2 tsp	freshly chopped sage
1 1/2 tsp	freshly chopped rosemary
425 g	ricotta
200 g	cheddar, shredded
250 g	freshly grated parmesan
1 1/2 cups	Dairyland Organic 2% milk
2/3 of 375 g pack	Prairie Harvest whole wheat dry lasagne noodles, precooked according to package directions
2 tbsp	bread crumbs

Serves 10

Nutrition Facts per Serving:
Calories 590, Carbohydrates 56g, Protein 30g, Fat 26g, Fibre 4g, Sodium 590mg

Method

1. Preheat oven to 350° F.

2. In a large frying pan heat 4 tbsp of olive oil on medium heat. Toss in shallots, cooking for 10 minutes, while stirring constantly.

3. Add pumpkin pulp and cook 10 more minutes while mashing pulp with a wooden spoon.

4. Pour in white wine and fresh herbs and continue cooking for 3 more minutes. Remove from heat.

5. In a separate bowl, mix ricotta and milk, then add 1/2 cup each of the cheddar and parmesan cheeses.

6. Brush remaining oil on the bottom of a 10-inch rectangular glass pan then sprinkle with 2 tbsp of bread crumbs.

7. Place one layer of lasagna sheets into the pan. Using a spatula, spread approximately 1 cup of pumpkin mixture evenly over the first layer of noodles. Next, sprinkle on a handful of the cheese mixture.

8. Repeat layering instructions above, making 4 layers. Ensure the top layer is pumpkin then sprinkle the remaining cheese on top.

9. Cover with foil and bake for 40 minutes. Uncover and bake for 15 more minutes until cheese is lightly browned.

Roasted Pumpkin and White Bean Dip

Ingredients

1	small, firm pumpkin
1	clove garlic
1/2 cup	Mum's Original hemp seeds
1/4 tsp	fresh ground pepper
3/4 tsp	sea salt
1/4 tsp	curry powder
1/2	lemon, juiced
1/2	lime, juiced
1	can white kidney or cannellini beans, drained and rinsed (392 ml)
2 tbsp	Mum's Original hemp oil

Serves 8 as an appetizer

Nutrition Facts per Serving:
Calories 170, Carbohydrate 12g, Protein 8g, Fat 10g, Fibre 4g, Sodium 300mg

Method

1. Quarter the pumpkin into wedges and remove seeds. Bake skin down on a cookie sheet for one hour at 395° F. Cool completely.

2. Scoop out 1 cup of pulp and set aside. Remaining roasted pumpkin can be used for pies, soups, etc. Also freezes well for future use.

3. In a food processor at high speed, process garlic and hemp seeds until smooth.

4. Add pepper, salt, curry powder, lemon juice, lime juice and beans and puree.

5. Add pumpkin and continue to process.

6. Add hemp oil and process approximately 30 seconds more. Check texture, when very smooth it is ready!

Serve with your favorite veggie sticks, baked pita chips, etc. Makes approximately 500 mL of dip.

Nutrition Tip: Hemp seeds, in addition to their omega 3 content, also contain a special anti-inflammatory omega 6 fat called GLA.

Marinated Flank

Ingredients

1	Diamond Willow whole flank steak (450 – 700 g)
1/4 cup	tamari, gluten free or regular
1/4 cup	Omega Nutrition balsamic vinegar
2 tsp	grated ginger
2	cloves garlic, chopped
3 tsp	dried oregano
2 tsp	fennel seeds
1/4 tsp	cinnamon
1/2 tsp	chili flakes
1/4 tsp	fresh cracked pepper
1/2	lemon, juiced

Serves 4 (based on 500 g of flank steak; 125 g per person)

Nutrition Facts per Serving:
Calories 210, Carbohydrate 4g, Protein 30g, Fat 8g, Fibre 1g, Sodium 1140mg

Method

1. Setting aside steak, mix all other ingredients together to make a marinade.

2. Lay steak in a long glass dish and pour marinade on top. Flip steak over to coat both sides with marinade.

3. Cover and refrigerate for a minimum of 24 hours and maximum of 3 days, flipping every 12 hours.

4. To cook steak, either heat the barbeque on high or heat a cast iron skillet over high heat and cook to just before desired doneness. Be careful not to overcook, basting steak with marinade on each side.

5. Allow steak to rest for 10 – 15 minutes after removing from heat.

6. Slice thinly on a 45 degree angle.

West Coast Strudel

Chutney Ingredients

1 tbsp	Omega Nutrition virgin coconut oil
1	red onion, diced small
1	small ripe pineapple, cored & diced into small cubes
1 tbsp	fresh ginger, diced small
1 tbsp	Camino Cuisine sugar
2 tbsp	dried cranberries
1/8 tsp each	ground cloves, ground coriander, ground cumin, and ground cinnamon

Cranberry Reduction Ingredients

7 tbsp	Camino Cuisine golden cane sugar
1 cup	100% pure cranberry juice, not from concentrate
300 g	organic frozen blueberries
300 g	organic frozen blackberries

Organic Brie Strudel Ingredients

3	small organic apples (or 2 large), washed, quartered and finely sliced (Fuji, Pink Lady, Gala, or Braeburn apples can be used)
200 g	brie cheese, cut into 16 pieces
454 g	frozen phyllo pastry dough, thawed (1 package)
1 cup	Omega Nutrition virgin coconut oil, melted

Makes 16 strudel

Chutney Method

In a heavy saucepan, heat coconut oil then add red onion. When onion is light and translucent, add pineapple, ginger, sugar, cranberries, and spices. Set aside.

Cranberry Reduction Method

In a heavy saucepan, heat sugar and cranberry juice. Reduce until 1/4 volume; liquid should coat the back of a spoon. Once reduced, add blueberries and blackberries. Warm and set aside.

Organic Brie Strudel Method

1. Preheat oven to 375° F.

2. On a flat surface, lay out one sheet of phyllo dough and brush entire surface with coconut oil (keep remaining sheets covered with a clean, slightly damp towel to keep them from drying out).

3. Place one piece of brie on the top center of the sheet and cover with sliced apple. Fold 1/3 of phyllo lengthwise over filling, then brush folded phyllo with oil. Fold opposite side of phyllo over filling, then brush with oil. Roll up and place on baking sheet.

4. Place baking sheet on middle rack of preheated oven and bake until phyllo is golden brown (approximately 12 minutes).

5. Place chutney in centre of plate and drizzle cranberry reduction around chutney. Place strudel (whole or cut in half diagonally) on top of chutney and serve.

> **Nutrition Facts per Serving:**
> Calories (per piece) 330, Carbohydrates 37g, Protein 5g, Fat 19g, Fibre 3g, Sodium 210mg

Our Partners

At Choices Markets, we are passionate about educating our customers and instilling an appreciation for where our food comes from. We would like to thank our generous sponsors for their dedication to making wholesome products to nourish our families.

Anita's Organic Grains

On Highway 1, just west of Chilliwack, BC – look hard for the simple sign marking Anita's Organic Grain & Flour Mill and retail market. In 2005, after 15 years of business, Anita and her family sold the business to a young local family, John and Dani MacKenzie. The brown bag eco-friendly packaging continues, as does their commitment to providing superior "pure and simple" ingredients, including ancient grains and flours like spelt and Kamut®. The MacKenzies' "what's important is what's inside" dedication provides high quality organic grains freshly milled and mixed locally into superior artisan quality flours and, more recently, a line of convenient, delicious whole grain mixes with no additives or preservatives.

Classic Smokehouse

Classic Smokehouse was started in 1996 as "Save on Seafood" with owner Stuart Dahlke as the sole employee. Combining his experience working with seafood wholesalers with his experience as a chef, Stuart began making unique smoked and raw natural wild BC seafood products. Thirteen years ago, Choices Markets became our first wholesale customer. Classic Smokehouse now employs over 30 people in a 14,000 square foot federally inspected facility on the Fraser River waterfront in Vancouver, where fish can be unloaded fresh from the catch. We purchase mostly from BC wild fishermen as we believe in supporting the fishermen and the fish they catch for all our futures. Our efforts have not gone unnoticed: we were voted "Best Smoked Seafood in BC by Canadian Living Magazine" by its readers.

Cocoa Camino and Cuisine Camino

The baking products that make up the Cuisine Camino® line are all fair trade, organic and support sustainable agricultural practices, local community development, and manufacturing by producer co-operatives. La Siembra, the Canadian worker co-operative behind Cuisine and Cocoa Camino®, purchases their brown sugar from the people of Cepicafé, a co-op of small-scale farmers in the northwest of Peru. Their golden cane sugar comes from Manduvirà, a producer co-op in southwest Paraguay. Cocoa powder comes from a farmer co-op-owned factory in the Dominican Republic. Connecting land and livelihood, local and global, Cuisine Camino® brings organic goodness to your kitchen.

Dairyland from Saputo

Shortly after his arrival in Montreal from Italy, Emanuele (Lino) Saputo persuaded his father, Giuseppe, to start their own cheese business in September of 1954. With $500 to spend on simple equipment and a bicycle to make deliveries, the Saputo family founded the company that bears its name. In the beginning, they produced 12 kilos of Ricotta and 12 kilos of Mozzarella daily. Today, Saputo is the largest dairy processor in Canada and the 11th worldwide, transforming over 6 billion litres of milk annually. Saputo markets and distributes Dairyland brand dairy products, continuing a 90 year long BC dairy tradition.

Diamond Willow

There are places on the earth that are unique. The Eastern Slopes of the Alberta Rocky Mountains is one of these places - a beautiful combination of visual scenery, productive land and ancient grass communities. We produce a pure, distinctive beef while protecting the fragile ecosystems that comprise these foothills. Cattle are grazed on foothill grasses during the summer months and wintered close to home. Our line of beef relies on a high level of management, not artificial inputs, to reflect the technology free status of the foothill range ecosystem. When this beef is ready for market, it represents one of the premium meat products in Canada, free of antibiotics and artificial growth hormones.

Farmcrest Foods

Farmcrest Specialty Chickens are raised on a family farm in BC's North Okanagan. Our family has over 50 years experience raising poultry to the highest humane and ethical standards. Our chickens are fed a traditional homemade all-vegetable diet of wheat, corn, soya, vegetable oil, vitamins and minerals, free of animal by-products, hormones and antibiotics. Most of these ingredients are grown right on the farm.

Having our own on-farm hatchery, feed mill, grow barns and processing plant means we are assured of the highest standards from the beginning to end which includes the elimination of trucking live birds.

Happy Days Goat Dairy

In 1993, Donat Koller moved from Zurich, Switzerland to Salmon Arm BC to pursue the quest of making the perfect cheese. Using his extensive knowledge of cheese-making, Donat applied his artisan skill to the goat dairy field to found Happy Days – a family run business. Quality starts from the very best ingredients, which is why only Saanen goats are used to produce the milk in our 100% Okanagan goat cheese rolls. Originating from Switzerland, Saanen goats are renowned for producing an abundance of high quality milk. Our goats roam freely, pasture in open fields and are raised without antibiotics or growth hormones. Healthy goats produce quality milk that, combined with our expertise, make Happy Days Goat Dairy products unique and delicious.

JD Farms

JD Farms is a family owned turkey farm in Langley, BC. Jack and Debbie Froese grew up on farms right here in the beautiful Fraser Valley and continued in their farming tradition when they purchased their own farm in 1979. With the help of their three children, Jack and Debbie grow Certified JD Specialty Turkeys year round. Turkeys on JD Farms are fed a natural diet of grain, vitamins and minerals – without any medications or animal by-products. The turkeys are raised in spacious, well ventilated barns with free access to fresh water and a constant supply of fresh feed. Each turkey must pass a stringent certification program which ensures our customers receive the very best!

LB Maple Treat

Company president Luc Bergeron started harvesting maple syrup in 1975 on a 52 acre farm located 150km south-east of Quebec City. During those early years he tapped approximately 5000 trees. Today his farm has grown to 1200 acres with 100,000 trees tapped, making it the largest independently owned farm in Quebec. All of our organic products are produced to meet the organic certification regulations and in addition we use sustainable, earth friendly farming practices. Our certified organic products are all produced without pesticides, antibiotics, hormones, herbicides, fumigants, artificial colorants, chemical fertilizers, preservatives or genetically modified organisms.

Lindsay Olives

The Bell Carter Family has been in the food processing business for over 90 years. Our commitment to bringing consumers the best quality food products began in 1912 and continues today. We continue to look towards the future, bringing innovation, passion and expertise to the olive category. Wherever the Bell Carter name is associated with a product, you have our assurance they are the absolute finest available. We would not have it any other way.

Mum's Original

At Mum's Original, it all starts with 100% organic Canadian hemp seed. Natural and organic ingredients are combined to make delicious nutrient dense foods that are easy to incorporate into your busy life. Our wholesome products are even more enjoyable knowing that our guilt free eco-packaging protects our children's future by accepting today's responsibility. Use our hemp seeds, hemp protein or hemp seed oil on their own or incorporate them into various recipes to revitalize meal time for the whole family...visit us at www.mumsoriginal.com for even more great recipe ideas!

Natura from Nutrisoya

Canadian owned and operated since 1992, Nutrisoya was founded with one goal in mind: to develop and produce the highest quality, best tasting products possible for your healthy lifestyle. Since 2002, Nutrisoya has concentrated its efforts on the development of innovative non-dairy soy and rice beverages. Nutrisoya's fully automated plant maintains the highest standards of hygiene, quality control, environmental protection processes and waste by-product recycling. Today Nutrisoya is a leader in producing delicious and nutritious non dairy alternative beverages benefiting from a ready supply of locally grown, certified organic soybeans.

Olympic Dairy

We promote health and wellness through food by producing the highest quality all natural and organic products, at affordable prices, for our customers. Olympic Dairy is a Canadian owned and operated manufacturer and distributor of premium all-natural cultured dairy, organic and soy products throughout Canada. We reflect a business ethic of integrity in all that we do and commit to providing excellent service to everyone we do business with. Our commitment to product value, quality and innovation is matched by our commitment to your health and the health of our environment.

Omega Nutrition

Omega Nutrition was the first company to introduce certified organic Flax Seed Oil to the North American market. Recognizing the critical need for essential fatty acids in the modern diet, founders Robert & Bob started their business in 1986 above the neon pink pig on Hastings Street. From these humble beginnings, they developed their proprietary omegaflo® process, which has set the industry standard for premium flax oil. They use only the highest-grade flaxseeds grown in North America; each lot is tested for flavor and quality. Omega Nutrition thanks their customers for making them a true homegrown success story.

Prairie Harvest

"Listen," said Vittorio Facchin's Italian friend, "if you want, you can have this pasta maker." In 1965, Italian immigrant, Facchin, accepted the simple gift with gratitude unaware of the success it would bring him. With that trusty pasta maker, Facchin worked from his garage and sold his authentic Italian pasta out of his car. Using only the finest ingredients and taking the time to slow-dry the pasta, Facchin's line of Prairie Harvest pastas quickly became a favourite among Edmonton's Italian community. Years later in 1996, Facchin's son Carlo, a second-generation pasta maker, took Prairie Harvest to new heights, establishing it as Canada's largest line of certified organic pastas. Since their humble beginnings in a garage, the Facchin family has branched out with their pasta line. Along with traditional pastas, the Prairie Harvest line also includes Artesian Acres Kamut pasta, San Zenone 100% wheat- and gluten-free corn and rice pastas and five great secret-blend sauce flavours.

Raincoast Trading

Mike Wick, the founder of Raincoast Trading, comes by his concern for the future of fish and their habitat legitimately. His family has been in the fishing business for four generations and he learned as a young boy to embrace environmental stewardship and responsibility. When Mike started Raincoast, he made a commitment to use only ecologically harvested fish. He also made sure that chain of custody procedures were implemented to trace every fish back to the boat that caught it. The commitment to quality extends to Raincoast's canning techniques – our fish is cooked only once, without water or oil to preserve the great taste and health benefits of this precious resource.

Sunrise Soya Foods

Sunrise Soya Foods humbly began as a one man operation in 1956 in Vancouver's Chinatown. Over the years, the company has grown to become the largest tofu manufacturer in Canada, employing over 200 Canadians at its plants in Vancouver and Toronto. Despite the company's success, Peter Joe, the founder's son and current CEO, has not changed his approach to business and his commitment to the community. All Sunrise, Soyganic and Pete's Tofu products are made with non-GMO soybeans from North American farmers. With no preservatives, all natural ingredients, no trans fats or cholesterol and the Kosher seal of approval, Sunrise is a healthy choice for you and your family.

Special Diets

Each of us is unique... and so are our diets! At Choices Markets, we are proud to serve a diverse clientele committed to caring for not only themselves but also the planet. As a result, our stores are filled with a world of options for those who want or need to eat a diet that is local, gluten free, vegan, low glycemic index, low sodium and everything else in between! No matter what your individual needs might be, our nutrition department, led by our resident dietitian, is here to help guide you on your healthy eating journey.

We wanted our cookbook to be no exception to our wellness philosophy; we believe cooking should be a joy no matter what your dietary needs are! For your convenience, each recipe is coded with coloured symbols to denote diet suitability:

Vegan   Vegetarian   Nut Free   Gluten Free   Detox Friendly

In this section, we have included healthy eating basics for our more common dietary requests. These pages are intended as educational information only and not to replace the care of a qualified health professional.

Looking for more nutrition information? You can always reach our nutrition team at www.choicesmarket.com/nutrition

Vibrant Health with an Anti-Inflammatory Diet

What does it mean to be truly healthy - just to be free of disease? We think not! Vibrant health means plenty of energy to live life to the fullest and a lifestyle that will help to prevent diseases such as heart disease, diabetes and cancer. Healthy food is critical for a healthy body and the right foods can help reduce inflammation, increase energy and prevent chronic disease.

What does a healthy diet look like?

The right approach to food: Food is not merely fuel – it is a social, cultural and emotional aspect of our lives. We must have a healthy relationship with food that strikes a balance between our nutritional health and our enjoyment of eating. Taking the time to prepare food and enjoy food is essential, as is avoiding extreme diet philosophies that leave you uninspired and lethargic.

The right amount of food: No matter how healthful the foods you choose are, overeating is overeating and it leads to weight gain. Once we gain weight, we enable negative biochemical changes in our body that exist independent of our eating patterns. Eat until satisfied, not stuffed!

Eat the right foods: Eating seven to ten 1/2 cup servings of fruits and vegetables every single day is by far the most important habit you can develop for your health. Produce contains the lion's share of vitamins, minerals, fibre and disease busting phytochemicals all in one low calorie package.

• choose dark leafy greens like broccoli, kale and spinach daily

• choose berries or pomegranate daily

• eat a variety of colourful foods: green, red, yellow, orange, purple – as each colour grouping has a unique nutrient and antioxidant profile

• Choose anti-inflammatory oils and proteins, avoid saturated and trans fats and keep animal foods like meat and dairy moderate in the diet.

• choose poultry and fatty fish like salmon, herring or sardines 2-3 times per week

• eat vegetarian proteins more often: beans, tofu and nuts

• make extra virgin olive oil your main cooking oil; avoid margarines and spreads

• snack on raw, unsalted nuts and seeds

• Choose whole unprocessed grains as often as possible.

• switch from whole wheat bread to sprouted grain bread

• choose whole wheat pasta

• eat "less processed" cereals such as steel cut oats or high fibre muesli

• experiment with unique grains like quinoa, buckwheat, amaranth, millet and barley

Try to avoid processed grains, added sugars and other high glycemic index foods such as cookies, crackers, sweetened drinks and snack items like granola bars as much as possible. Finally, cook with plenty of fresh herbs and spices and enjoy antioxidant rich green and rooibos teas often.

To learn more, read Ultimate Foods for Ultimate Health by Liz Pearson RD and Mairlyn Smith and Eating for Optimum Health by Andrew Weil MD.

Special Diets: Vegetarian

What is most commonly referred to as a vegetarian diet is one that excludes meat or fish but may include dairy and eggs.[1] This dietary pattern offers a great deal of flexibility and many of the health benefits of vegetarian eating such as lower risk of heart disease and cancer.[1] While vegetarian eating can be healthy, not all vegetarian foods earn a gold star – potato chips and ice cream are vegetarian too! Common pitfalls on this diet include relying too heavily on dairy for protein and eating too much saturated fat as a result; eating too many snack foods and not enough fruits and vegetables.

Protein is an important part of everyone's diet and vegetarians are no exception. Including a source of protein at each meal and snack will keep you energized and stabilize blood sugar levels. It is important to note that while vegetarian proteins often lack one or two essential amino acids, it is not necessary to protein combine at each meal.[1] Eating a variety of grains, beans, eggs, dairy, seeds and nuts throughout the day will ensure that you receive all the essential amino acids you need.

Low levels of iron and zinc can be another concern on the vegetarian diet. However, research has found that the body adapts to a vegetarian diet to improve iron levels in the long term.[1] Vegetarian sources of iron include dark leafy greens, fortified breakfast cereals and milk alternatives, beans and dried fruit. Fermented products like tempeh and sprouted grains or beans are more bioavailable sources of both iron and zinc. Combining iron-rich foods with a source of vitamin C such as berries, peppers or tomatoes improves absorption. Another helpful hint: avoid taking calcium rich foods like milk or supplements with iron rich meals as calcium can impede iron absorption.

Meat eaters and vegetarians alike need to watch their intake of Vitamin D – the only substantial food source of vitamin D is salmon. Recommendations are 1000IU of vitamin D3 daily – ask your health professional if this is right for you.

Finally, think about your omegas — alpha-linolenic acid is the omega 3 fatty acid found in plants. Try to choose 2 servings of omega 3 fatty acids in your diet daily.[2] Choose from hemp, chia or ground flax seed, walnuts and canola oil. DHA supplements from algae are also available.

Want to learn more? Read The New Becoming Vegetarian by Vesanto Melina RD and Brenda Davis RD.

1. Position of the American Dietetic Association: Vegetarian Diets. J Am Diet Assoc 2009;109:1266-82

2. Messina, V., Melina, V., Reed Mangels, A. A new food guide for North American Vegetarians. Can J Diet Prac Res 2003;64:82-86

Special Diets: Vegan

Whether for health reasons, environmental or ethical concerns, vegans choose not to consume any animal products. As a result, vegan diets exclude dairy, eggs and other animal products such as honey and gelatin. While this diet pattern is a bit more restrictive than a vegetarian one, vegans can have wonderfully varied and healthful diets.

Plant-based diets are gaining in popularity and are becoming an increasing focus in nutrition research. Fruits, vegetables, whole grains, nuts and seeds are the cornerstone of any healthful diet. Rich in essential vitamins and minerals, they are also loaded with fibre and antioxidant phytochemicals. A vegan diet pattern typically has much higher levels of fibre and antioxidants and much lower levels of saturated fats. [1] Vegans also enjoy lower rates of obesity and chronic disease such as heart disease.[1]

In addition to the nutrient concerns described in the vegetarian diet section, excluding all animal products proves a challenge in getting adequate calcium and vitamin B12. Vitamin B12 is found only in animal foods so an alternate source of B12 is essential for vegans; Red Star nutritional yeast and fortified milk alternatives are the most convenient sources of vitamin B12.

Bone mineral density is often lower in vegans,[1] so paying attention to your calcium and vitamin D intake is essential. The calcium in 1-2 cups of a fortified milk alternative or fortified orange juice will help you reach your daily needs more easily. Interestingly, the calcium from bok choy and broccoli, two lower oxalate greens, is even more bioavailable than that found in milk.[2] When it comes to vitamin D, it is important to note that vegans are at risk for deficiencies of vitamin D.[1] With all we are learning about the health benefits of vitamin D, a daily dose is essential. The preferred form of vitamin D – vitamin D3 - is vegetarian but not vegan as it is derived from lanolin.[2] Vitamin D2 is derived from yeast but may not be as bioactive.[2]

As a vegan, food preparation can be a breeze. There are an increasing number of food products available to the vegan, from coconut milk ice creams to veggie pates. Explore vegan websites and magazines and discover innovative recipes that make eating a joy.

Want to learn more? Read Becoming Vegan by Vesanto Melina RD and Brenda Davis RD

1. Craig, W. Health effects of vegan diets. Am J Clin Nutr 2009;89(suppl):1627S-33S

2. Position of the American Dietetic Association: Vegetarian Diets. J Am Diet Assoc 2009;109:1266-82

Special Diets: Low Sodium

The Canadian Hypertension Society estimates that over five million Canadians have high blood pressure.[1] Think that high blood pressure is no big deal? High blood pressure is actually the leading risk factor for death in North America, according to the World Health Organization.[1] While blood pressure control is a multi-faceted approach including diet, exercise and stress reduction,[2] keeping sodium out of the diet is vital.

Food manufacturers are flooding our food with salt so that we keep eating and eating. The average Canadian eats 3500mg of sodium each and every day.[1] To prevent high blood pressure, stick to no more than 2300mg of sodium a day; if you already have high blood pressure, 1500mg is the recommended target.[2] One teaspoon of salt is about 2300mg of sodium but simply avoiding the salt shaker is not enough! More than 80% of the sodium in our diets comes from packaged and prepared foods, some of which might not even taste salty.

Here are some high sodium culprits you may be unaware of:

• Olives and pickles

• Condiments such as ketchup

• Fast food like hot dogs and pizza

• Frozen prepared dinners

• Breads and baked goods

• Canned soups, fish and vegetables

The easiest way to cut salt out of your diet: cook from scratch! When you cook at home from fresh ingredients, you have total control over the salt content. We have included the sodium content for all of our recipes so that you can cook with confidence.

When at the grocery store, smart shopping is in order. Shop the perimeter of the store and make fresh whole foods – fruits, vegetables, lean meat, dairy and unprocessed whole grains - the core of your diet. Here are some other tips to help you shop low sodium:

• Look for the "low sodium" claim on packages – "reduced sodium" items such as soups may still be too high in sodium.

• On the label, meal items with less than 400mg of sodium per serving size are the way to go – but watch out for sneaky "too small" portion sizes.

• Choose canned fish and beans without added salt or be sure to rinse salted versions well.

• Select lightly salted snack foods and choose raw nuts and dried fruits over salted and roasted trail mixes.

Want to learn more? Visit www.sodium101.ca or www.hypertension.ca

1. Hypertension Society of Canada. Accessed on August 4 2009 at: http://www.hypertension.ca/

2. 2009 CHEP recommendations for the management of hypertension. Accessed on August 4 2009 at: http://hypertension.ca/chep/wp-content/uploads/2009/01/2009-chep-recommendations_d3.pdf

Special Diets: Nut Free

Nut allergies are rising in our population, making many schools and homes nut-free zones. As nut allergies can be life threatening, it is important to be diligent in making food choices for your family. Thankfully, food manufacturers are responding to consumer demand, making their facilities peanut and nut free; some companies go as far as making kid-friendly snacks free of all major allergens.

Peanuts and tree nuts are not related to each other but both are common allergens in Canada. Allergic reactions occur in response to a specific protein in the food. Food sensitivities, on the other hand, result from a different mechanism in the body and usually do not cause life-threatening reactions.

Making nut-free choices at the grocery store requires careful label reading. Products with the peanut free or nut-free claim have gone the extra mile in testing to assure that no traces of the allergen can be found in their product. However, this is still a relatively small portion of the market. For all other foods, check the ingredients and look for an "allergen warning" statement that might say "contains peanuts" or "may contain traces of peanuts" or even "processed in a facility that also processes nuts." These are your clues that the food may not be safe for your family. Avoiding of bulk bin items is also recommended.

On the ingredient label, items to watch out for include imported foods with hydrolyzed plant protein, arachis oil, vegetable oil, or Valencias for peanut allergy and marzipan and gianduja chocolate for tree nut allergy. Pay close attention to snack foods, ice creams and chocolates. Ensure your home is completely free of the allergen to prevent not only cross contamination of other food items but also accidental ingestion. What about substitutes for good old fashioned peanut butter? Several varieties of nut butters exist, from almond to cashew. For those who must avoid all nuts, soy butters and sunflower seed butters are also available.

When dining out, beware of African, Thai and Chinese cuisines that may have widespread exposure to peanut or nut. In addition, deep fried or pan fried foods may be cooked in peanut oil as it has a high smoke point. Always alert the service staff at a restaurant to your allergy.

Want to learn more?
Visit http://www.anaphylaxis.org/ or http://www.hc-sc.gc.ca/fn-an/securit/allerg/fa-aa/index-eng.php

Special Diets: Nutritional Detox

Our bodies, in their innate wisdom, have the remarkable capacity to heal. However, modern lifestyles and environmental aggressors start to overwhelm this healing capacity resulting in fatigue, skin problems and weight gain. As the years accumulate, a host of chronic diseases may follow. While periodic detox will not totally compensate for years of ill health, it does provide an opportunity to rejuvenate the body's natural healing processes and can act as a catalyst for making permanent dietary change.

Several popular detox kits exist but gentle detoxification through appropriate diet, exercise and relaxation is also possible. Such lifestyle programs also make detox accessible to those on medications who would not be able to take herbal preparations. However, as with any major dietary change, no matter how temporary, be sure to seek guidance from your health professional before commencing.

Traditionally, nutritional detox consists of the following principals:

• Avoiding wheat and dairy

• Avoiding all added sweeteners, processed grains, refined flours and alcohol

• Avoiding yeast and fermented foods such as black tea, soy sauce, vinegars

• Avoid foods which may harbor moulds such as mushrooms, peanuts and melons

• Limit high glycemic foods such as dried fruit, juice or tropical fruit and starchy vegetables such as potatoes

For a gentle nutritional detox, we recommend daily intake of these foods:

• Plenty of dark green leafy vegetables and other non-starchy vegetables such as tomatoes and carrots

• Low glycemic fruits like berries, apples and pears

• Lean protein such as eggs, chicken, fish, tofu and beans

• Unsweetened non-dairy beverages like soy, almond or rice

• Whole, unprocessed grains such as brown rice, quinoa, steel cut gluten-free oats and buckwheat

• Raw nuts, seeds and their butters

• Organic plain yogurt to create a healthy intestinal environment for cleansing

• Plenty of filtered water and herbal tea such as rooibos to support elimination

Our cookbook includes detox friendly recipes which may or may not adhere to the guidelines outlined in other programs. For example, some practitioners allow goat milk dairy foods and suggest avoidance of all major allergens, including soy or avoidance of "nightshade" plants. Our detox friendly recipes are all free of wheat, dairy, processed grains and added sweeteners. If you have other guidelines, these and many other recipes in the book are easily adapted: substitute lemon juice for vinegars or omit added wine or cheese.

Special Diets: Gluten Free

Gluten is everywhere – not just in the bread aisle! Gluten is a storage protein found in wheat, barley, rye and their derivatives, including spelt and Kamut. On a gluten-free diet, most commercially available oats also have to be excluded as they are cross-contaminated with gluten.

Without gluten, what's left to eat? If you shop at Choices Markets —plenty! Eliminating gluten from your diet requires know-how and patience but there is a whole new gluten-free world opening up on the grocery shelf. Many of the healthiest foods — fruits, vegetables, beans, lean meats and dairy, nuts and seeds — are naturally gluten free! Gluten-free grains include quinoa, rice, corn, amaranth, millet and teff, which can all be found baked into breads and pastries, ground into baking mixes and even used as a base for frozen pizzas and cookie dough.

Even trickier is watching for hidden sources of gluten, which include everything from soy sauce and other condiments to ice creams, snack foods and even dried fruit. To help you avoid gluten containing ingredients, Choices Markets offers a gluten free product listing and a tagging program on the shelf to help you spot gluten free goodies at a glance. For more information about our gluten-free program, speak with a member of our nutrition team. When picking up your groceries, be sure to read every ingredient label and refer to the Pocket Dictionary of Acceptability of Foods and Food Ingredients for the Gluten Free Diet, available from the Canadian Celiac Association.

Following a strict gluten-free diet will ensure that your gut heals and that nutrients are absorbed properly. Once you have figured out your gluten-free routine, focus on some key nutrition areas. Celiacs are at risk for low iron, vitamin B12 and folate. Eating fortified foods will help reduce your risk of deficiency. Celiacs are also at risk for osteoporosis, so eat calcium-rich foods and consider taking a vitamin D supplement. Choose whole grains as often as possible and eat high fibre beans, fruits and vegetables daily. Remember, just because that cake is gluten free doesn't mean it is healthy!

Want to learn more? Visit our website for our Gluten Free Living handout and read The Gluten Free Diet by Shelley Case RD - a one stop shop for everything you need to know about eating gluten free.

Index

Dessert
    Chocolate Ricotta Tartlettes, 104
    Creamy Maple Rice Pudding, 18
    Gluten Free Chocolate Pudding, 132
    Gluten Free Vegan Chocolate Fudge Cake, 39
    Harvest Cherry Crumble, 66
    Omega Rich Sweet Treats, 43

Dips
    Mojito Chutney, 93
    Pumpkin Seed Hummus, 29
    Roasted Pumpkin and White Bean Dip, 138
    Smoked Cheddar Dip, 116

Duck
    Polenta Medallions with Caramelized Duck, 120

Eggs
    Spinach and Feta Frittata, 31

Fall
    Artichoke and Quinoa Stir Fry, 97
    Buckwheat Crepes, 98
    Chocolate Ricotta Tartlettes, 104
    Clover and Cucumber Salad, 87
    Escarole Salad with Warm Dressing, 94
    Granny Smith and Zola Salad, 89
    Green Lentil, Kale and Spinach Soup, 84
    Greek Style Wilted Mustard Greens, 83
    Hearty Millet Soup, 95
    Kamut Penne with Eggplant, 109
    Lentil Coconut Soup, 85
    Maple Salmon Croutons with Roasted Tomato Salsa, 92
    Millet and Romaine Wraps, 80
    Mojito Chutney, 93
    No Egg "Egg Salad", 107
    Onion and Tomato Beef Stew, 105
    Pasta with Hemp and Cheddar Pesto, 101
    Potato and Artichoke Tart, 90
    Roasted Local Chicken and Veggies, 91
    Smoked Herring and Heritage Grains Salad, 81
    Sprouted Red Wheat Tabouleh, 86
    Squash and Orange Soup, 100
    Tuscan Squash Risotto, 99
    Vatellina Style Cabbage Rolls, 82
    West Coast Yam Chowder, 106

Fish
    Asian Salmon Curry, 51
    Bigoli and Tuna, 41
    Fettuccine with Salmon and Fennel, 50
    Kasha and Salmon Cakes, 125
    Maple Salmon Croutons with Roasted Tomato Salsa, 92
    Mediterranean Halibut Bites with Pesto Dressing, 21
    Mediterranean Style Stuffed Potatoes, 122
    Mustard Crusted Salmon, 72
    Salmon and Watercress Salad, 65
    Smoked Herring and Heritage Grains Salad, 81
    Swiss Steak of Salmon with Radish Salad, 60
    Tuna and Brown Rice Wrap, 40
    West Coast Potato Salad, 47

Greek Style Wilted Mustard Greens, 83
Jerk Chicken and Potato Salad, 57
Mediterranean Pearl Salad, 73
Mushroom and Mustard Seed Salad, 25
No Egg "Egg Salad", 107
Pasta and Chopped Veggie Salad, 35
Radicchio, Fig and Orange Salad, 67
Salmon and Watercress Salad, 65
Sprouted Red Wheat Tabouleh, 86
Smoked Herring and Heritage Grains Salad, 81
Summer Bean Salad, 53
Tunisian Salad, 61
West Coast Potato Salad, 47

Spring

Baked Brie and Sun Dried Figs, 20
Beef Salmonato, 36
Bigoli and Tuna, 41
Braised Brisket and Leeks, 45
Carrot and Zucchini "Flowers" and Shiitake Caps Stuffed with Goat Cheese, 34
Creamy Maple Rice Pudding, 18
Chick Pea and Arugula Salad, 44
Citrus and Wild Mushroom Fettuccine, 23
Easy Coconut and Chicken Soup, 46
Gluten Free Vegan Chocolate Fudge Cake, 39
Italian Brown Rice with Arugula Pesto, 19
Mediterranean Halibut Bites with Pesto Dressing, 21
Mushroom and Mustard Seed Salad, 25
Omega Rich Sweet Treats, 43
Pasta and Chopped Veggie Salad, 35
Portobello Melt, 28
Pumpkin Seed Hummus, 29
Spinach and Feta Frittata, 31
Swiss Chard Wraps with Yogurt Pesto, 32
Tofu and Shiitake Stir Fry, 33
Tuna and Brown Rice Wrap, 40
Turkey Breast with Grapefruit and Mint, 24
Turkey and Veggie Meatballs, 37
Tofu Scaloppini, 42
West Coast Potato Salad, 47

Soups

Asian Turkey Chowder, 115
Basic Vegetable Stock, 52
Blue Russian Potato and Corn Soup, 131
Chilled Roasted Tomato Soup, 54
Cream of Mushroom Soup, 130
Easy Coconut and Chicken Soup, 46
Green Lentil, Kale and Spinach Soup, 84
Hearty Millet Soup, 95
Lentil Coconut Soup, 85
Onion and Tomato Beef Stew, 105
Squash and Orange Soup, 100
Summer Peach and Coconut Soup, 77
Sunchoke Soup, 114
Turkey and Shiitake Summer Stew, 74
West Coast Yam Chowder, 40
Winter Beef Soup, 133
Winter Vegetable Stew, 113

Summary

Summary